Jon Cornick

About the Author

CONCETTA BERTOLDI is the *New York Times* bestselling author of *Do Dead People Watch You Shower?*, which has been translated into seven languages. A consultant to members of the royal family, celebrities, and politicians, among others, Concetta has appeared as a guest on such programs as *The Early Show, Today, Good Morning America, Bloomberg TV,* and at live events and seminars across the country.

Born November 18, 1953 in Newark, New Jersey, Concetta is the middle child of three children. Born with the inability to hear in one ear, she has communicated with the Other Side since childhood, and as a young adult she was tested and identified as "clairsentient." In 2001, Concetta left her mainstream job to go public and work as a medium full-time. She has embraced her abilities and has learned to share this glorious gift with others.

Please visit her website at concettabertoldi.com.

ALSO BY CONCETTA BERTOLDI

Do Dead People Watch You Shower?

DO
Dead People
WALK
Their
DOGS?

QUESTIONS
YOU'D ASK A MEDIUM
IF YOU HAD THE CHANCE

CONCETTA BERTOLDI

HARPER

NEW YORK · LONDON · TORONTO · SYDNEY

HARPER

HarperCollins books may be purchased for educational, business, or sales promotional use. For information please write: Special Markets Department, HarperCollins Publishers, 10 East 53rd Street, New York, NY 10022.

FIRST EDITION

Library of Congress Cataloging-in-Publication Data
Bertoldi, Concetta.
    Do dead people walk their dogs? : questions you'd ask a medium if you had the chance / Concetta Bertoldi. — 1st ed.
        p. cm.
ISBN 978-0-06-170608-0
1. Mediums.   2. Future life—Miscellanea.   I. Title.
BF1283.B465   2009
133.9′1—dc22   2008040727

13   OV/RRD   10 9 8 7 6 5 4

In loving memory of my mother, Eleanor Hackett Ferrell,
an amazing woman, who survived a horrific childhood and
beat the odds to become a beautiful wife and mother. I will love you
and thank you forever.

INTRODUCTION

When I accepted an offer to write and publish my first book, there was no title that immediately came to my mind. As the one answering the questions, not asking them, it was hard to know what to focus on—there would be so many subjects covered, so many stories, that I couldn't really think of anything that from my perspective really "said it all." But when I sat down with my editor and agent to toast the new deal, it turned out they both were thinking the exact same thing. I have to say I loved it right away, and since the book has come out I've heard from so many readers how much they love it, too! People from all over have written to me, or sent e-mail messages, about their encounters in the shower and other places with some very lively ghosts.

Really, this concern about ghosts seeing us naked completely cracks me up. If it's not the shower, people are worried about spirits looking over their shoulder (and other body parts) when they're in bed. It really makes me wonder what they're doing that they're so concerned! What? Are they afraid that cops will break down their door waving handcuffs and shout, *"Cut that out right now! We just got a complaint from a dead person!"*?

A woman named Diane sent a message to my website:

Many years ago (twenty-five, to be exact) I went to see a medium for the first time and was going to ask about a cross-country move. She immediately asked if my father had crossed over and I was shocked and said yes, and told her that I was uncomfortable because now I will think he is watching me all the time. She said, "He says, 'Don't worry—not in the shower.'" I laughed because she had pinpointed his personality with that comment.

Needless to say, the title of my book piqued Diane's curiosity and she found herself picking it up!

It's hard to express how exciting it's been to see my first book come out and to have it be so well received. I don't know why writing a book was so important to me—a dyslexic who has always had trouble reading. But I've always loved books and have bought and read so many by other mediums over the years, especially when I was trying to make sense of my own abilities. And I've long collected books on Marilyn Monroe, who I adore. So books have always been special to my heart. Having my own opened the doors to meeting so many more of you through shows I did at some really wonderful bookstores and libraries—RJ Julia bookstore in Connecticut; Book World in Caldwell, New Jersey, where more than one hundred people showed up even though it was pouring rain and flooding so badly you practically needed a boat to get there (I told my husband, John, that only ducks would show up, but I was wrong); The Book Loft in Hackettstown, where the crowd exceeded the store's capacity and we had to go across the street to the Comfort Inn; Book World in the Rockaway Mall; and the Borders in Wayne, to name just a few of these fun events. And now the book is being published in other countries, too! When John and I were traveling last year in Germany, I was browsing a book shop in Frankfurt and suddenly I "saw" my book there, in that store. I'm sure many a new author has had such a daydream, but lo and behold, when I got back home, my agent called to tell me that German translation rights had just been sold, so my vision would soon become a reality!

Even though I'm psychic, I never could have predicted what I've been seeing lately as an incredible, growing acceptance of the truth that we never really die. Even ten years ago this idea would have been considered "fringe." Now everywhere you look there are books, TV shows, and movies whose subject is the Other Side. Sure, some of them still portray it as someplace eerie, populated with evil spirits, for the sake of entertainment, but many now take a more realistic perspective, that there truly is nothing to fear. With this growing popularity, people are more comfortable thinking about the Other Side and that seems to have opened a floodgate of questions.

One area that I don't think I covered well enough last time concerns our dear four-legged friends. As you probably guessed from the title of this book, I want to get to a lot more questions about our beloved pets this time!

So, here I am again to answer even more questions about the Dead, tell more stories that I've been witness to or that my clients have told me, share more of my karmic experiences with my friends and relatives. Yes, my mother-in-law is still a rock in my underwear. Yes, she still treats me like a bastard child at a barbecue. But to put a spin on Abraham Lincoln's famous words: You can please some of the people some of the time, you can even please most of the people most of the time, but you can't please all of the people all of the time. Just can't be done, so get over it. But before I drop the subject, I have one thing I must say about my mother-in-law: For eighty-five years old, she looks fabulous! She really is beautiful. It's true. I have to declare it.

Okay, we've got a lot more questions to get to here, but before I move on I just wanted to say that it was never my intention to make anyone afraid to pick up the soap. I was in King's, a grocery store in Boonton, New Jersey, one day and a woman came up to me and said, "Are you Concetta Bertoldi?" I said, "Yes," and she said, "Well, thanks to you, I always shower with one eye open now!"

Me? I pray in the shower—I'm not worried about it. God knows it all anyway.

Can the Dead joke with us?

One time I was doing a reading at one of my big shows and the questioner's mother-in-law came through. Unlike my own situation with *my* mother-in-law, they had been very close. Most of the time I can validate who the spirit is by asking them the means of their crossing, how they died, which the person is able to confirm. But in this case, her mother-in-law didn't want to talk about that at all. She kept saying to me, "Just say T—she'll know what it means." Well, I sure didn't know what it meant. Was it an initial of somebody? The first letter of a place? Who knew? But the spirit was insistent so I told her, "She's saying to just mention the letter T and you'll know what it is." She looked puzzled. She said to herself, "T? T?" then she laughed. She said, "Oh! I get it! Tea! Like you drink, a cup of tea. After my mother-in-law died, her daughters and I had to go empty the house so it could be sold. In Mom's kitchen were boxes and boxes and boxes of Lipton's tea! No English Breakfast or peppermint or Darjeeling or chamomile. No. Every time we opened a cupboard, there was more Lipton's tea! My sisters-in-law and I still laugh about how much tea Mom had." Clearly they weren't the only ones laughing—her mother-in-law on the Other Side was enjoying the joke, too.

I think even souls who were very sober when they were here lighten up when they get to the Other Side. We're all different so not every dead guy is a comedian, but when they see the big picture they just get a little lighter. And they appreciate it when we can be lighter, too. I had four women come to see me for a group reading. They didn't look anything alike so I was guessing they were friends, not sisters. It didn't take long before I saw, standing behind all four of them, the spirit of a woman who told me she had died of cancer. When I asked why she was claiming all of them, did they know who she was, they all nodded somberly and told me that she had been a well-liked coworker of theirs named Viola. Viola had a big smile for one of the four women and I said to her, "Why is it that Viola is telling me that you were the funniest one of the bunch? And what is it she's showing me, like this?" I picked up a pen that I'd been signing books with and pointed it at her. Finally that got a smile out of her. She told me that while Viola was still able to work, sometimes she'd have a pretty bad day and to get her out of her mood she would shoot rubber bands at her with her pen. If Viola was having a *really* bad day, she'd take the whole box of rubber bands and empty it on Viola's head! So silly, but such a loving gesture at the same time—we all appreciate that kind of thing, don't we?

Why is it that mean, rich people keep on getting richer?

If we're just looking at the external evidence, it sure can seem that life is not fair! So it shouldn't be surprising, I guess, that this is one of the questions that I'm asked most frequently. Why does this guy who treats everyone so badly get the promotion and pay raise? How come that nipplehead wins the Mega Millions or the 50-50? Why doesn't it go to somebody who really deserves it? He doesn't even need it! What's up with that? Well, the guy who got the promotion might have been kissing up to the boss, for one thing, but I know what you mean. It always seems like those who have, get more, and are frequently the least deserving. But the answer is this: When you see someone who looks like they have plenty and doesn't even appreciate what they have getting more, you can be sure that it's God giving them another chance to learn a lesson—what it's like to be generous, to help someone less fortunate. That's the simplicity of the Other Side—if we're paying attention, we get opportunities over and over. God doesn't need our gratitude; *we* need to experience gratitude. We need to experience sharing.

When we share, what we receive back is so much greater than what we've given. Some people never seem to learn that one. But God keeps giving them chances. I don't know if there's ever a point where, if the lesson is ignored or failed over and over, that God will cut them off—at least for this lifetime. I'm just not sure about that. Being human, I'd like to think He would, but that's me making a judgment—*I'd* cut 'em off—and that's not my job. That's His job. None of this stuff we have here belongs to us— not our cars or our clothes, our homes or our cash. All we have that is real is our love for God and for each other. If we don't express our love by sharing our so-called material possessions with others, we're gonna get an F on that test and the next lesson is guaranteed to be a harder one.

We also need to practice generosity of spirit, to be giving of ourselves, not just of what we have. We need to make a circle of sharing. People who have trouble receiving attract people who have trouble giving.

Why is it that mean kids who bully others don't always get their comeuppance?

I think it's pretty similar to the guy who needs to learn about sharing. They've got lessons to learn! At least if it's a kid behaving in such an unkind manner we can hope that they will wake up sooner rather than later. I think we all know people—I've seen it go both ways, those who learn and those who don't. I have a client whose history of bullying I know more than a little about. I didn't know him when he was a child, but it's not hard to imagine that he was a mean little kid and never grew out of it. He was horrible to his wife all their lives together, demanding, controlling, wouldn't let her drive, made her wait on him, yelled at her. He was completely abusive to her. Then his wife was dying, and as she lay in bed she wouldn't even look at him; all she was focused on was knowing that soon she'd be free of him. She said good-bye to her son, but would not even speak to him; he couldn't understand it. She crossed over, leaving him here in his own bad company. Now he begs me for readings, he has all kinds of regrets, he feels sorry for himself, but it's too late for him. He isn't gonna get what he wants on this side anymore.

On the other hand, when I was a kid, there was a boy in our class who was very big, hefty for our age. He was a real brat. His size let him push other kids around and he made the most of it. Then, when he was around fifteen or sixteen, his sister died and everything in his life was just shattered, it was such a blow to him. That loss made him change. It taught him the real values, what is important, and ever after he became just the sweetest, nicest person.

I don't want anyone to be confused. In neither case do I believe God was meting out some punishment by taking away someone who these individuals loved. (I'm sure even my client believed he loved his wife, even though he made her life such misery.) God's not about punishment; when one's wife and the other's sister crossed, it was their time to do so, in accordance with their own karma, for reasons known only to God and that spirit. The point I'm making is how one woke up and changed and the other apparently won't in this lifetime.

It's never too early to consider the karmic debt we are taking on when we treat others unkindly. (By the time a kid is about thirteen, if not sooner, they should be able to understand this, and many very young children simply know it instinctually.) Or, conversely, the karma we burn away when we treat others with kindness. When you see that rotten kid who picks on someone different from them or weaker than them and getting away with it, God is giving them another chance to show kindness, and if they are lucky, they'll open their eyes, realize how wrong their behavior is, and become a much kinder adult, aware of and grateful for the extra chances they got.

God also is giving anyone who witnesses such bad behavior an opportunity to champion the child who is being picked on. We're all in this together—it's rare that behavior like this goes on behind a curtain, so to speak, away from other eyes. Any one of us can offer friendship or protection to an underdog.

The last thing I'd like to say about this is more for the younger person who maybe hasn't been around the block as often as some others of us, and that is, remember that the misbehaver will always want you to join them. If they can get you to join them in their bad behavior it makes them feel better about themselves.

Believe me, someone doing crack will only be too happy to hand you some, too. I was at a wedding one time and at the reception this girl who looked like she was about seventeen was drinking alcohol and was frankly drunk. She wasn't yet suffering from the guaranteed hangover she was going to have, so she was very "happy" and pleased with herself for her condition. Of course, then she hooked up with a thirteen-year-old and started in trying to convince the younger girl that she should be drinking, too. She went up to the bar and got another drink and put it right in the girl's hands. That's just the way it is. And someone being mean just loves it if they can get someone else to be mean as well. When someone tries to get you to engage in any kind of act that you know is wrong—whether it's wrong toward another person or just wrong for you—you need to be strong, be yourself, don't get confused about who you are or let them confuse you into thinking that their actions are right for you. You need to be your own person.

How do the Dead let us know that they hear us, or let us know they are there?

There is really no limit to the different ways that those on the Other Side show us that they are always around us and know that we are thinking of them. They might keep showing you a particular time on a digital clock. (I know one woman, for example, who many more times than would be a natural average will feel compelled to look at her clock right when it says 11:11.) A lot of times they will arrange for events to be connected with unusual timing that will make us look at the event in a different way. That's one thing I'm eager to explore when my time comes (though I can be patient about it!)—finding out how exactly they do this. But to give you an example, I had a couple come in, a brother and sister, and after the reading the brother told me he was very impressed. That made me feel good—I never get tired of hearing I'm doing a good job. Then he told me he had been a skeptic. Their mother had died five years before, and three years ago, his sister had made this appointment. He'd told her at the time that he didn't believe in psychics and she could go to the appointment if she wanted, but he wanted nothing to do with it. Eventually, the three years passed, and about two months before the appointment was scheduled, he had an incredibly vivid dream. In it, his mother was saying to him, "Go! Go! Go!" The dream was so real that he felt it was important to do what his mother was asking but he had no idea what it was. He got in his car and drove out to the cemetery to visit his mother's grave and talked to her, asking her to tell him what she wanted him to do, where she wanted him to go. Not hearing anything, he was frustrated. He decided to go see his sister and tell her about the dream and see if she had any idea what it meant. He had just finished describing how his mother had told him emphatically to "Go!"

One of my clients, a young woman in her twenties, told me that her cousin had died when she was only twenty-three after having an epileptic seizure in the middle of the night, bonking her head, and suffocating in her pillow. A few years later, after reading my first book, she was in a grouchy mood, and feeling skeptical about whether it really was possible to communicate with her cousin's spirit, she decided to do an experiment. She thought for a while about her cousin, then, in her head, she said, "Okay, Jamie, if you're really hanging around me and care about me and are now enlightened, give me a sign. Show me a sunflower." (Sunflowers were her cousin's favorite flower.) The next day, she was reading a book and she came across the word "sunflower" on the very first page. The following paragraph talked about an "encounter with transcendence." Later that day, she told me, she saw a man carrying an armful of sunflowers. And that night, she saw a new TV commercial that flashed over a whole field of sunflowers.

My client's grandmother had an experiment of her own going. She had pictures of Jamie all over her bedroom, and apparently for a year after her granddaughter's death no matter how often she straightened the pictures, she'd always find them crooked.

Another of my clients, "Jim," told me that when he'd started his landscaping business his father sometimes helped him with a job. One day they were excavating a job, making holes to put in shrubs and trees, when he dug up a box full of old bottles, in perfect condition. Jim was no bottle expert; he just thought they were cool looking and thought possibly they might be worth something. (He later found out that they dated from the early 1900s.) Without a lot of room at his own place, he asked his dad if he could keep the bottles in his garage. Eventually, he forgot about them. Then one day he was at a flea market and he saw bottles like the ones he'd found being sold—they were really pricey—and, remembering that most of what he'd found was in better condition than those the flea market vendor had, he got excited. He went back to his parents' house, only to discover that at some point the bottles must have been thrown out or given away. Even though he realized these things happen, Jim was annoyed, and whenever the opportunity came up, he never failed to mention to his dad the valuable bottles that had been *entrusted* to him and that he'd gotten rid of. Since Jim's father has crossed over, a couple of things have happened. First, again while digging on a job, Jim found an old milk bottle with the name "Alfred" written on it—his father's name. On a separate occasion, Jim found another bottle. It had dirt caked all over it, but when Jim washed it off, he found the letter A. He said, "Concetta, do you think this is my father trying to get my bottles back to me?" Absolutely. Jim's father found a very distinctive way of letting Jim know he was still around.

Yet another client had a daughter who had died and she would go from time to time to visit her daughter's grave. On one occasion, after she'd spent some time at the graveside, she walked back to her car. Getting in she noticed she was holding a broken necklace in her hand. She definitely had been distracted, so thought she must have just idly picked it up off the path without even realizing what she was doing, because she really didn't have a clear memory of having bent down and picking it up. She was shocked to see that it had letters spelling out Kathy, her daughter's name.

The important thing is for us to notice. Especially if we've specifically asked them to show us some sign, but even if we don't ask, we still need to keep our mind open to them, knowing that they will be trying to say hello to us in any way they can. Keep reminding yourself there's no such thing as a coincidence, and realize that when these things happen that might ordinarily make us go "wow!" or "cute!" it's most likely someone who was dear to us trying to let us know they are nearby.

Is there one method that the deceased use more than others when they want to connect?

I don't know what it is about dead guys, but they love the radio. This seems to be one of their preferred methods of sending a hello to us here. I've heard so many stories from clients, I'll just give you a handful here. . . .

A man who is a client—real sweet—and a hairdresser said to me, "Concetta, why don't you let me do your hair sometime?" So that's what we were up to when he told me this story. He said the first time he came to see me, he was a skeptic. His mother, whose name was Rose, had died when he was thirteen and his sister was fourteen. He himself was gay, but years later his sister married and had a baby. One day, as his sister was driving her child to a pediatric appointment she found herself talking to her mom in her mind, wondering whether her mother had known her baby, or was aware of her here. Just then, an old song by Seal came on the radio, "Kiss from a Rose." His sister smiled, thinking what a sweet coincidence; she wanted to share it with her brother, so she called him at work. When my client picked up the phone, he had the radio on, too, but a different station. Just as his sister was telling him about this funny coincidence, hearing a song with Rose in the title just when she was talking to her mom, the very same song came on the radio in my client's shop! Double whammy! By the time he heard from his mother in our session, he was no longer a skeptic!

One young woman came to see me with her mother and her

mother's Aunt Rose came through—more roses!—and she kept saying something about rags. I know that sounds weird, but I don't make the stuff up, I just try to communicate what I hear to my clients. They couldn't figure out what she was talking about, what rags had anything to do with. I told them, "Don't worry, it's being recorded. You can listen when you get home and it'll probably come to you." They left my office puzzling the mystery. It didn't take long. By the time they got out to the car, the mother said, "I've got it! I know what Aunt Rose was trying to say. Remember when you and your sister were little girls, she used to put your hair up in rags to curl it—she always said you two looked like a pair of little rag dolls! Thinking of Aunt Rose, the mother and daughter decided to drive through the old neighborhood where they hadn't been in about twenty years. They were driving along with the radio on, reminiscing, and just as they were going past Aunt Rose's old house, on the radio came Frankie Valli's "Rag Doll."

Another client, Mike, told me, "You know how certain memories stand out and stay with you, even when they don't seem really a big deal? Well, when I was eleven years old, I remember driving with my grandparents in Fairfield. I remember, there had been some plane crash, and on the radio was this Bon Jovi song 'Always.'" The song, that day, and his grandparents just stuck in his head together, and it was one of those odd memories that would resurface for him from time to time. He went on to tell me that last year his grandmother had died. He went to the funeral, and as he walked in the funeral procession, he was thinking of her and asked her to give him some sign that she was still near. Afterward, he got in his car to drive home and on the radio comes that very song, "Always."

If we want to get a message to a loved one who has crossed over, how can we know that our message has been received?

It has been told to us that what is asked is given. We have God's word on that. If you want to be sure your message goes through, just ask that of God. Whether you do that in prayer, or softly spoken out loud as you walk in a favorite place, or just with the words in your head, it doesn't matter. God knows. That's really all you need to do.

Is the Day of the Dead the real deal? Do the Dead really come back to life?

It is the belief in Mexico, and a number of other countries around the world, that November 2, *El Día de los Muertos*, is the Day of the Dead, when all those who have died come to life. In some places November 1 is called *El Día de los Angelitos* (the Day of the Little Angels), and those who have lost a baby will remember him or her on that day and deceased adults on the second. People will carry flowers and the favorite foods of the deceased to their grave sites and leave them there for the Dead to enjoy this special meal. (For children they would leave toys and traditional candies.) If it's not possible to travel to the grave site, they'll set up a small desktop altar with photos of the deceased—very often there will be a cross or religious statue, maybe of a saint, or a picture of the Blessed Virgin Mary, flowers (especially marigolds, which are considered especially significant for this remembrance), candles—and set out the foods they liked best, and maybe a bottle of tequila or other spirits. A popular decoration that also is a treat are little skulls made of sugar or chocolate, which symbolize death and rebirth. Day of the Dead celebrations are very old—they can be traced back nearly 3000 years to the Aztecs, Olmecs, and Zapotecs, among other indigenous groups. More modern versions of the celebration are carried out in Texas and Arizona in the U.S.

Different countries also celebrate their deceased loved ones, in a variety of ways. In Guatemala, they make and fly huge kites. In Haiti, drumming and music are a big part of the celebration— they play very loud all night—to literally awaken an entity they recognize as the god of the Dead. In Bolivia, the Dead are remembered on November 9 and the celebration is called *El Día de los Natitas*, the Day of the Skulls. Each home usually has the skull of an ancestor who watches over the family and on that day they get it all gussied up, adorning it with flowers, and make offerings of food, cigarettes, and coca leaves, among other things. The Chinese do things completely differently with their Qingming Festival ("Clear and Bright" Festival). They celebrate in the springtime—usually April 4 or 5—by making time to enjoy the outdoors and the fresh new greenery of the new season, and at the same time, tend to the grave sites of their loved ones.

But to get back to the original question about the Day of the Dead specifically, the Mexican people have always been extremely in touch with family—both living and dead. But after the revolution of 1910 any overt spiritual expression of this kind was driven underground. Apparently the government considered it backward or superstitious, even though individual politicians honored their own dead relatives in this way. The fact is, you can suppress this kind of loving expression, but you can't kill it. It might have been publicly "unacceptable" but it still was practiced behind closed doors, so to speak. And not only on November 2, when all the Dead are honored. An individual family member will also be remembered on the anniversary of their crossing. The family will gather and decorate the home with flowers and photographs of the deceased. There may be an urn with the deceased's ashes present if that person has been cremated rather than buried. The family will enjoy a meal of their loved one's favorite foods. Sometimes this is a simple and reverent family dinner; sometimes it's a full-on party.

As I'm always saying, the Dead are *always* with us, not just the second day of November. But that is a day set aside when they are given special remembrance, honor, and celebration. Do they literally come back to life? They are always *literally alive* in spirit form.

What do you think about Halloween?

Halloween is a very old celebration in other parts of the world. In this country, it's mostly just a nice holiday for children—they carve pumpkins, dress up in costumes, have parties, go trick-or-treating, and come home with too much candy. But as far as a holiday goes, Halloween wasn't even really celebrated here until the last century. It wasn't any kind of big deal. We had some good innovations—in Ireland they used to carve a face into a turnip; we used a pumpkin, which is a helluva lot easier to get a candle into and make stand up on your porch! But the more important days here, in the Christian tradition, are All Saints' Day on November 1 and All Souls' Day on November 2, when the "faithful who have departed" are celebrated. It's funny, because *El Día de los Muertos* in Mexico has much more traditional "weight" to it, but now in Mexico the celebration of American-type traditions of this holiday is catching on and children there will dress up and go door to door, saying—instead of "Trick or Treat!"—"*Noche de brujas!*" which means "Night of Witches!"

When I was about five or six years old, my brother Harold and I had these cheap store-bought Halloween costumes—the kind that are all one piece, you step into them and tie them at the back of the neck. I can't even remember what mine was, but Harold's was a red devil suit. Harold, eleven months older than I, was simply petrified of his mask. He was crying and crying and my mother, who was trying to get us out the door to a party, said, "You don't have to wear it." And as young as I was, I remember saying to him, "That can't hurt you." I don't know how I knew, and I didn't really even have the words to express it, but I knew that he was a blessed child and that nothing evil like a devil could harm him. I understood this, even that young, even though I couldn't say exactly what I meant.

Does Great-Grandma hate my piercings?

If someone is a decent human being and does the right thing in their life, the Other Side isn't going to look at your tattoos and piercings and make some contrary judgment. To them all the things we do over here on this side to make ourselves either stand out or blend in are just amusing. I personally like to wear a lot of big jewelry, but mostly in not very original places on my body. If somebody else wants to get more creative with it—stick seven earrings on this ear, a dozen on the other, a hoop or two on their belly button, their nose or wherever else (believe me, I've heard of some *very* creative places some people have pierced, but I don't really want to mention those)—Grandma Over There doesn't care. Grandma here might because maybe she doesn't understand it, or maybe thinks it will reflect badly on the family or whatever. But over there, they realize that it's not such a big deal. If you have tattoos all up and down your arms, Grandma Over There might wish you'd wear long sleeves when you go to work, but that's just because she'd be concerned that people here might judge you and it might keep you from being taken seriously and advancing in your career or whatnot. It has nothing to do with her personal feelings that you shouldn't have tattoos.

How does a medium know if the information she is relating to clients is true?

Well, for one thing, usually whoever I'm doing a reading for is able to confirm what I am telling them right then. Bear in mind that I'm only repeating what I'm hearing, I'm not making stuff up. Even if it seems like it, I'm not. As an example, I have a client whose mother died, and she came to see me three times. Both the first and second time she came, her mother mentioned, along with a lot of other stuff, the name Helen. My client insisted she had no idea who Helen was, but clearly this was someone significant to her mother, especially as she repeated the name on both occasions. As I said, it's her mother saying Helen, not me. Still, I could tell that my client had doubts since she was sure that anyone close to her mother she would have known or at least have heard of. Finally, the third time this woman came to see me she said, "Oh, Concetta, I found out why Mother keeps mentioning Helen! I was going through some of my mother's things and I found a ring inscribed inside 'To Helen from John.' Along with the ring was a card addressed to my mother that said, 'I'd like you to keep this,' so at least that part of the mystery is solved." Even if we don't know, the souls know what they're talking about. I say prayers that I'm only passing along the good stuff. I trust my prayers and I trust the souls. The souls over there on the Other Side are really where the credit goes for "getting it right." They're so darn good, they could talk a dog off a meat truck! Not all are witty; some are as boring as some people here. But I *trust* them!

Do dead people ever lie?

No. They have no reason to lie. What are they going to get out of it? First of all, communication is all telepathic on the Other Side and you can't get much more transparent than that. Everybody knows what everybody is thinking so lying would be pretty impossible. Kidding? Yes. Joking? Yes. But lying? Not possible. Now that I think of it, since telepathically we all understand one another, maybe over there we'd even be able to get all the dumb jokes that didn't make sense to us before!

If there was a person who had lied or betrayed someone when they were here and then crossed over, it's not like they'd come through with a full confession or explanation of their behavior. They might possibly be able to convey a couple key details to me about the situation, but it's far more likely that they would just express remorse or say they were sorry.

What is the absolute strangest place you've ever been visited by a dead guy (or gal)?

I was in a restaurant bathroom one time, sitting in the stall, peeing, when a spirit started telling me she had a message she wanted me to give to her sister. This was around 1981, and I hadn't gone public yet. Even though I have a naturally flamboyant personality I wasn't really "out" yet and didn't feel that comfortable just saying to a stranger, "Hello, I'm a medium, and I have a message for you." Anyway, I finished my business, pulled up my drawers, and when I came out of the stall there was a girl standing at the sink washing her hands. I gathered my courage and said, "Excuse me, is your name Cheryl? Or something that begins with a C?" She said, "It's not Cheryl, it's Cathy, but I do spell it with a C." I said, "Okay, well, I feel the need to tell you something. Your sister wants you to know that she loves you." To be honest, I can't remember exactly her reaction—whether she was shocked or a little bit disbelieving. All I recall is that she said that it was very nice to know it because her sister had died recently and they'd had an argument just before and she'd been feeling bad about that.

Do the Dead miss their favorite foods?

In spirit form we don't consume anything—nothing to eat, nothing to drink. It's just not necessary as we are noncorporeal (a fancy way to say we have no body). However, we do have our memories of wonderful meals we've had, and certainly we'll also remember fondly our favorite foods. At one of my shows a spirit came through for his family and he was telling me to ask them about some cookies they had with them. I said, "Did you bring some cookies with you, in honor of your dad?" They at first looked puzzled and then realized that they did have some cookies in their bag and they laughed. They hadn't been thinking of him; they had just put them in there in case they wanted a snack. But he'd been aware of the cookies and that's how he was letting them know it was really him because he'd been known when he was living for his sweet tooth.

Do the Dead concern themselves with the health of their living loved ones?

Absolutely, they do, in every way. It might be in a reassuring way, in that they will want to tell a loved one that their worries are for nothing, that some health crisis they are experiencing will end well. Or it might be cautionary. Very often I will have a spirit ask me to convey to a client that they don't want them to smoke, or they'll tell them to get some exercise. When I was around forty-seven or forty-eight, I was in a bar for happy hour at the end of the work week. At the end of the bar was a young guy with a bunch of little girls hanging around him. Well, not really "little girls," but you know—it's all relative—they were younger than me. As I sat there, just kind of taking in the scene, I heard a dead guy talking to me; he wanted me to go talk to the guy at the end of the bar. It was his father, and he was insisting that I go talk to the son. He was telling me that he was an alcoholic, and he wanted me to tell his son that he didn't want him to be drinking in a bar. To be honest, I really, really didn't want to just go up to some guy who had no idea who I was and try to tell him something like that. But the father was very insistent.

Finally, I knew I had to do it. So I went down to where this guy and his friends were and I said, "You don't know me, but I'm a psychic medium, and your father gave me this message for you, and he's been really insistent that I pass it along." I told him what his dad said. I said, "He's telling you he's sorry for the way he was.

And he doesn't want you to do this." It was awkward, to say the least. Afterward, I just went back to my seat.

A little bit later, I stole a look down the bar and I saw the young guy with his head down on the bar, and his girlfriends were around him like, "Are you okay?" I felt a little bad, but I had to tell him what I was hearing. Anyway, after a while, his friends came over to me and were asking, "Who are you?" They told me he was really upset. Then they told me the story, what he had told them. His father had been a serious alcoholic, wreaking havoc with the family. After one episode, the young man had said to his family, "That's it. I'm done with you. You're not my father!" Right after that, the father had again gotten drunk and got into an accident and was killed. The young man was feeling so guilty that he'd disowned his dad and then his dad had died. Out of guilt, he was drinking himself into a stupor, and probably an early grave—just like his father. The father, naturally, was upset. He wasn't mad at his son; he understood. But he was worried and wanted to give his son a warning, any way he could.

If I'm having surgery, can my dead loved ones help me?

Yes, anyone we love who has crossed over becomes part of our team of guardian angels, so to speak, and they will be helping in any way they can. Over there, they are all-knowing and they are with God; they are one with God, so both they and God will be with you.

Keep in mind you are going into a subconscious state so you will be more readily able to connect with spirit—anesthesia won't in any way impede this. If anything it'll help because you are taken out of your normal waking focus on the physical plane. Try having some small item with you that symbolizes your connection with God and spirit, however you think about that, whether it's a prayer card with Mary Mother of God, a star of David, or a small statue of Jesus or Buddha, or Michael the Archangel or whatever makes you feel at peace. It can also be some small item that reminds you of another person, especially someone who is now in spirit form. (I have a small thing that belonged to my brother Harold that I use.) Assuming that you feel comfortable leaving this item unattended and that it won't be taken, place it next to the bed you will be in to recover. You don't really need this item; it is only symbolic, an acknowledgment of your peace of mind. Then simply ask that the Other Side be with you, tell your guardian angels that you want their comfort, and that you want to wake up well and strong.

When someone is under anesthesia, where does their soul go, and can they connect with loved ones on the Other Side?

Yes, they certainly can. The reason is, when we are in a semi-conscious state our conscious mind is at rest and our unconscious mind is heightened. In this state it's very easy to connect with spirits. We are able to slip out of the body—this is our soul in its pure energetic form—while remaining connected by a cord of energy. In this form, we connect with other non-physical energy forms like our deceased loved ones, who are able to give us reassurance for the healing process.

Can the Dead literally save us when we are in life-threatening circumstances?

Yes, of course they can. This happens all the time. For instance, I often get messages telling my clients to check certain things about their cars—like, maybe there's a problem with the brakes or something. The dead person is trying to keep their loved one from having a bad accident. And I frequently hear stories about how a deceased loved one saved one of my clients from hitting someone or being hit, just in the nick of time. Recently one of my clients told me that her cousin, whose sister had died, was driving dangerously on the highway. In an instant she missteered and was losing control of the car, doing over 80 miles per hour. She was headed straight for a concrete barrier when she saw her dead sister standing right in front of her car wearing the dress they buried her in. The next thing she remembers is being safely stopped on the grass about a dozen feet or so away from the barrier. This type of situation is actually pretty common.

My own eight-year-old grandson Alexander is such a handsome, beautiful boy. He calls John and me Grandpa and Grandma Pickle because one time when we were visiting, John was being annoying, and I said to him, "You are such a PICKLE!" Alexander thought this was the funniest thing, and he just laughed and laughed. So ever after, that's who we were to him. But to get back to my story, in spite of our funny nicknames, I could never understand why Alexander never seemed to warm up to me. I'm pretty approachable, if I do say so myself, but he always seemed to be a nervous boy and kept his distance.

The fact is, it turns out that Alexander has always been able to see spirits, he's always been visited, and they actually scare him. Also, he clearly is aware that other people are not seeing what he's seeing. About two years ago he finally said to his mother, Darlene, "What would you do if I told you I see things?" Darlene asked him, "What do you see?" He explained to her that he was seeing people, ghosts. I always say to people—and Darlene has heard me do this spiel many times—"Don't show fear. If you show fear, then the visits will go away." So Darlene said, "Well, you know, Grandma Pickle sees them, too!" Well, ever since then Alexander has been all over me. He knows that we share this ability and he knows that I will never think anything is strange if he tells me what he sees.

One time, his sister Julia, who is six, fell down the steep basement stairs, landing on her knees on the concrete floor. Because she was startled, she cried. Darlene was scared to death. She yelled, "Oh, my God!" and ran to gather up her little girl, thinking they'd be making a trip to the hospital—or worse. But there was literally not a mark on her. She was completely fine. Alexander, who had witnessed the fall and seen the spirits intervene, told me, "They put her down. They held her when she fell. You believe me, right?"

And many years ago, when I was only four months old (this is a story my mother told me) and my brother Harold was fifteen months, he fell out of a third-story window in the Newark projects where we were living. It was a terrible accident—he hit each cement windowsill on the way down and landed smack on the concrete sidewalk below, breaking virtually every bone in his body. The ambulance came and took him and he was pronounced dead at the hospital. He had a tag on his toe that said

Baby Ferrell. My mother was beyond distraught—she was only twenty-two years old. She felt guilty, like the accident was her fault, and of course she couldn't bear to think that her child was dead. My grandfather on my father's side had the same ability that I have, and he said to her, "Don't worry. He'll make it, and he won't have any sign of the accident." How that could be possible only the Other Side would know. My mother at that time didn't really know anything about my grandfather's psychic abilities— it wasn't talked about in the family. She probably thought my grandfather was crazy. She threw herself across Harold's little body, and as she did so, she saw a tiny tear in the corner of his eye. She cried to the doctors, "Please, check him again!" They did, and were amazed to discover that he wasn't dead after all. Harold spent six months in the hospital, but just as the Other Side had predicted, he had no lingering problems, not a mark from having fallen three stories and broken all his bones.

What happens in cases of accidental killings? Are they considered murder?

First of all, I would have to say no, but this is one of the hardest questions because, as you know, I don't believe there is any such thing as a coincidence (something unusual happening for no reason at all), so I have to say that in each case of an accidental death, the person who dies knew that their life this time would end in this way. Maybe they did not know the exact circumstances, but they would have agreed to leaving at or around that age in order to effect a particular lesson—not for himself, necessarily, more likely for the individual who caused the accident—and they would have been aware of at least a general idea of the reason. Each major circumstance of our lives has karmic reasons attached to it. It's playing out an event to balance another previous event, and to offer a lesson to those involved. This is not to say that the person who is killed is conscious, while they are still on this side, that this is the plan. And the person who causes the accident also believes it was an accident, at least most of the time, even though they have made an agreement before coming here to play this very sad role. To everyone involved, the death appears to be an accident. I just know from all my experience talking with the Other Side that it's not what it appears.

I've had the experience more than once of doing a reading for someone who had found themselves in this type of circumstance. In one case, it was a man who had inadvertently killed one of his coworkers with a piece of heavy machinery. In another case that I remember too vividly, a mother was completely devastated because she had accidentally run over her two-year-old toddler, who got behind her car as she was backing out. I felt so helpless in that reading. I couldn't get out of my own way because I was so strongly relating to her pain. I couldn't tell her strongly enough that God knew her pain and confusion, that this was for a purpose. To her, it was an accident, yet the guilt she was suffering was unbearable. In my heart, I know her child's death in this way was not coincidental, but what the purpose was, what the lesson was, I cannot imagine.

In the case of an airplane crash or serious train accident where many people die all together, is that also "preplanned" on the Other Side?

Yes, and again, there is always a reason. Nothing is for nothing. In a case like this where one accident takes many at the same time, there will be particular karmic reasons for each individual, and at the same time, these people will have shared karma as well. They will know each other on the Other Side and through many other lifetimes. An event like this has layers of meaning. It's not just about the pilot or conductor or the individuals on the plane or train. It's also about others in their lives who will be affected by each person's crossing in one way or another. You can call it a ripple effect or a domino effect. It could be an event like 9/11 or a bus being blown up by a terrorist. It doesn't stop with those individuals, that event, that day—the effects go on for entire lifetimes, plural.

I should say that there are also karmic reasons for each person who "missed their plane" or "usually rode that train" but didn't that day. Nothing is a coincidence. A coincidence is nothing more than God remaining anonymous.

What is true spirituality?

True spirituality is living in partnership with God and relying on that spirit to come through, guiding our thoughts, our words, our actions. More than any other power of any kind on Earth, God is the greatest. His love is greater than logic, greater than money, greater than muscle.

Personally, I have not achieved true spirituality. I don't think I'd still be here if I had. Everyone here, with very few exceptions, is still working toward it. The frustration is when I know right from wrong and still can't stop myself from doing wrong. That's the place I'm in, in this particular lifetime. I know in my heart the difference, yet I'm human, not divine, and I still make mistakes. They say ignorance is bliss, but I'm not ignorant. I don't have bliss.

Do dead people walk their dogs?

The souls on the Other Side are with their dogs—or cats, or ferrets, or whatever creature they cared for and loved here. However, their beloved animals never have to be on a leash. The Other Side is a place of perfection. It's not survival of the fittest over there. We walk among the "savage beast," and they walk with us. It's absolutely natural for us to grieve the loss of a beloved pet when he or she crosses over. Especially people who don't have children or live far from family or friends—our pets really *are* family to us—and maybe I shouldn't say this, but in some ways possibly even dearer, since who can resist being loved without any strings attached? But it's true, those creatures we loved while they were here will be reunited with us in Heaven.

Will all our pets be with us in Heaven, or just our favorite ones?

Our pets are gifts from God and God's gifts don't just disappear into thin air. All go back and all will be there.

If there was one pet we loved best of all, will our other pets be okay with that or will it hurt their feelings?

They'll be thrilled! You have to remember that the Other Side is total perfection. It's only here that we harbor petty jealousies. Nothing of the kind exists over there. ALL creatures rejoice with God ALL-mighty.

I think I may have psychic abilities and my church does not really approve. Is there any reason to fear these abilities?

It's so interesting to me that it always seems to be the things that we don't know or understand that we're most afraid of. It's hard for me to talk about this because it does cross the line of some people's religious beliefs, and I do feel that everyone is entitled to believe what they want, worship how they want, so long as no one is harmed by their beliefs or the way they worship. But I do feel that if people knew what I know of the Other Side, they would realize that it doesn't take anything away from religion. This ability, like any other ability, comes from God. God is all-powerful and all-providing. There is nothing we have here that doesn't come from God, so that must include my ability (or yours!) to have a connection with spirits who have crossed to the eternal realm beyond the life of the physical body. We just tend to fear what we don't know—whether it's dying or waiting to get the results of a test. Or sometimes, just the terminology makes a difference between what's acceptable and what is "bad" or "not allowed." For instance, it may be true that certain religions will not be accepting of a "psychic," but they are very comfortable with the idea of a "prophet." And just to be clear, I am not, not, *not* calling myself a prophet! But as I understand it, a prophet is one who receives a message somehow—sometimes in a dream or another way that the Bible doesn't even make clear—and can tell what is going to happen, or receives and passes along a tiny part of what God's plan is for a particular person or group of people at a particular time. The message may be different, usually more important than the kind of message someone like myself might hear from a client's deceased family member. But the means may not be that different. I can't tell you how many times one of my clients will share with me that they had a powerful dream that made them understand something or warned them of something or gave them some message that they needed to hear—and these people don't even consider themselves psychic, much less prophets! Sometimes the messages I get are things that my client can act on, that may protect them in some way, but oftentimes they really aren't. They are just confirmations that the spirit is who they say they are because they know things the client can confirm. So I admit that the importance of the message is really limited to just that person, but still it isn't harmful in any way, and I have to assume, on the face of the evidence, that the intention behind a loved one on the Other Side communicating in this way is to make that person here feel better.

I think, basically, people just need to learn to make the distinction between good psychics and lousy ones, instead of lumping everyone together. Even in the Bible, God warns against false prophets, right? So use your sense. If you see a big red neon hand that says PSYCHIC READINGS $5, or run into someone who would tell a client that she needs to bring them a wheelbarrow full of cash, or a toaster, or a pillow case, or whatever you might want to think twice. There's a good chance that individual is a charlatan, or as I call them, a "boardwalk psychic." I wish I could give a more definite answer to this, but I really don't want to place myself in opposition to someone's religious beliefs. It would be like I'm saying, "I'm a higher authority," to contradict what someone's church was telling them. All I can do is speak for myself to say that, as God is my witness, in my heart, I am only trying to do good, only positive, loving work with the ability I've been given. I think if you have this ability, that is the test you should give yourself. After that, personally, I don't care what name anyone gives me or what I do so long as it's not negative.

Is there any sure way to get rid of negative energy in one's home or around one's person?

We really don't need any smudging or perfumes or candles or anything. The best way I have found to do this is to focus on the light of God inside myself and ask the spirit of perfect love—which is God, after all—to wash my body and home, inside and out. Just ask God. Call it a prayer, if you will. I call it spiritual hygiene. It's not for special occasions or circumstances; I do it regularly, like brushing my teeth or showering. Spiritual hygiene—I don't know if I invented that, but I like that expression.

Can psychics play the ponies?

Can they? Maybe. Maybe they could get away with it at first. But actually, I doubt it. I'm very firm in this: Whether or not they *can*, a psychic *should not* play the ponies. I don't feel that my ability is a gift that is given with "no strings attached." I think it comes with responsibilities. There's the saying, "To one whom much is given, much is expected," and to me this means I need to be the one to police my own behavior and try to do what is correct with the ability I've been given. I always know when it's appropriate to ask for something and when it's not. The truth is that the Other Side always knows when I need something. This is really true of everyone, but I think my unique experience has made me a lot more aware of this than most. When I really need something, I know the Other Side will help me to get it. By "need" I mean that my getting it—whatever it is—will be attached to some higher good. Is my winning a million-dollar lottery attached to some higher good? Not really. It's just money. But there's a huge difference between my wanting a certain horse to come in first at the Meadowlands because I've got a bet riding on it, and, on the other hand, my wanting my book to be successful because the messages in it are important for people to hear.

Does God know if we "covet our neighbor's wife"—or husband, for that matter?

God knows all things so I, personally, wouldn't try any sneaky stuff and think I was getting away with it. This material plane is such a place of trials and challenges. It's not perfection like the Other Side, and it contains every sort of temptation. We're all here to learn and I, for one, cannot pretend to know the nature of someone else's lessons. Sometimes I don't even know my own until a long time afterward. So I don't want to be holier-than-thou with this question. It's not my position either to condone or to judge what someone else does. I can tell you this, though: If someone made a move on John I would definitely have something to say about it—she'd get a whole lot more than she bargained for! Outside my own relationship, in cases where I maybe hear something through the grapevine, I make an effort not to judge. In a situation that I'm not directly involved in, I try very hard not to have an opinion. That's God's business.

If someone had an affair and was never caught, would their significant other find out about it once they crossed to the Great Beyond?

Oh, definitely, they'll know the truth. They'll know everything. And once they are on the Other Side, that knowledge won't hurt them. Forgiveness is big business over there. However, that does not at all mean that this betrayal was meaningless. And it doesn't mean that those involved will be getting off scot-free. No such luck. Actions like this don't just affect the two involved in it and their significant others—they affect many people connected to the two in a variety of ways and karmically can take a long time to balance out.

Why do some psychics use cards or a crystal ball to do a reading?

Speaking strictly from my own experience, when I first went public, I used to lay out Tarot cards just to take the attention away from myself. They were literally a decoy. I was afraid that without the cards people would judge me or think I was strange because I was hearing or seeing something that they couldn't hear or see. I was afraid they wouldn't believe me. Reading cards seemed like something more tangible. A big problem, though, was that I didn't really know how to read cards. I'd never learned what the different symbols meant. It could be embarrassing because every now and then I'd get a client who knew a lot more about them than I did. She'd go, "But doesn't that card mean the house of love?" and I would have no clue what she was talking about, so it could get me in hot water. It seems funny now that I'd put myself in that position and actually thought it was better than just telling the truth. But eventually it got to the point where I wouldn't even remember to look at the cards, so my cover was pretty well blown. The interesting thing was that the cards were, for me, a step. I don't like to say "a crutch"; actually, they were more of a tool to get me from one place to the next. They helped me build confidence because even though they weren't the source of the messages I was giving, they allowed me to do my thing as a new professional and get confirmation from my clients that the messages were real. Once I didn't need them anymore, or saw they were just getting in the way, I took the deck off my table.

It's funny because there were some return clients who actually were disappointed when I stopped using the cards. They really liked the cards and could not be convinced that to me they were meaningless. That said, there are some people who seem to be really talented in interpreting the various symbols in the cards themselves or the way they end up being laid out, depending on the shuffle. I think that is a true talent. But I also feel that people who are very good at that must also have good old ordinary psychic ability without the cards. I personally can't see how cards themselves could have any real power.

How is your psychic style different from other mediums?

I can't pretend to have experienced too many other psychics lately, but I visited quite a few in my twenties when I was trying to come to terms with my own abilities. In many cases there seemed to be more rigmarole than necessary. I tend to connect with a spirit and get their point fairly rapidly, even when it's more of a puzzle I'm putting together. Also, if a client wants to reach a particular person, I *nearly* always can reach them. I realize that I might come across as flippant to some, but I deliver. Everyone's personality is different. It's no different for us—mediums are people, too. I like to say that the way I work is like a short-order cook. Just tell me what you want and I put it in the window. Some of the others are like bad foreplay—you could do without it, it doesn't amount to anything, it's just annoying. You want to say, "Just get to the point."

What are some ways the average person can increase their psychic capability?

It's really so simple. I've said before, we are on the brink of a time when more and more people will be tuning in to this and other abilities that today seem extraordinary. Just look at our popular culture—the ideas are out there now, all around us, and reality always follows the ideas. Everything is mental before it becomes material. Children will develop these abilities much more rapidly than adults since kids don't have any other job than just to learn their world. What we call the psychic—seeing, hearing, and communicating with spirits who have crossed to the Other Side—is already a real part of a child's world. When that reality is affirmed by the parents instead of being ridiculed or denied, the child won't lose that. It's really the parents who have the most to learn, but as I said, if you look around you see that every day now, we're learning more about these realities.

One thing I do that helps to center me and keep me in open contact with God and the Other Side is to practice meditation. Finding some time in your day to quiet yourself, breathe deeply, and open yourself to that connection can be really helpful. In a focused way, express the desire to be in contact with your guides. Maybe visualize yourself opening a window to let in the Other Side.

Basically, we need to practice awareness. We need to tune in to the instincts God gave us, listen for the little voice that runs alongside our own in our head, pay attention to the different feelings we get in our body that inform us of other levels of truth going on around us all the time. Even though there can be a playful nature to our psychic abilities they aren't primarily for our amusement. The main reason we have this is for our protection and our soul growth: in other words, to learn our lessons. A classic example would be if you are in a shop and your own mind is telling you something like, "The manager just walked into the backroom. I could put those earrings in my pocket, pay for my chewing gum, and walk out—nobody the wiser, and I've got a cute new pair of earrings." Then that other voice that is there to protect and teach you says, "Don't do it, honey. You don't need 'em that bad. Even if you don't get caught, they'll always remind you of a moment when you were dishonest and you will never enjoy them."

Even if you don't think you are especially psychic, virtually every single person can think of at least a few times when they had a strong feeling that they needed to avoid a certain person or stay away from a particular place or situation. This feeling was nothing more or less than their sixth sense, what some call ESP (extra-sensory perception), which essentially is a form of being psychic, but instead of cautioning us about our own behavior, it's warning us about someone else's behavior. I can think of several occasions where I used this very ordinary kind of ESP in my own life.

For example, sometime before I went public I was working at a famous sporting goods store. There was a guy, Willy, who worked in the service department. I always got a vibe from him that he was a little odd. I knew there was something wrong with him, but didn't know exactly what. It bothered me, but there was nothing I could do about it since he always just seemed to be doing his job. One day I was driving and I saw Willy with a little boy; they were both wearing baseball uniforms. Suddenly I "knew" that Willy was a child molester. Now I was really upset, wondering what I could do. I knew it, but there was no way for me to prove it. But then I heard in my head the Other Side saying to me, "A conclusion is coming." I realized I had to just let things play out without my intervention and just trust that the right thing was going to happen. It was only a short time after that that the boy's parents found letters written to their son. They were actually from Willy, but they were written like they were from someone else. The boy had been very, very upset by the things that Willy was doing with him and had tried to break away from him. He was refusing to see Willy and Willy was trying to get him back under his sway. The letters were along the lines of "If you don't go with Willy, I'm going to kill your parents." Crazy, horrible stuff. When the parents found the letters, they easily put two and two together and went to the police. Willy was picked up and pleaded no contest and went straight to jail. Granted, in this case, I had the added assurance of hearing from spirits that "a conclusion was coming," but my original impulse—straight from the gut, garden-variety sixth sense—was that there was something not good about this person. He was poop on a plate, and now he's where he belongs—poop behind bars!

Are children more psychic than adults?

I do think this is generally true. Lots of kids have bits of memories of who they were before in other lives, for instance, and they're very tuned in to spirit. They know a lot more than they are given credit for about who means well and who doesn't—generally speaking they have good ESP because they were only a short while ago on the Other Side and have not had enough time here to be tarnished. They still have their good listening ears on.

When I was just a very young girl, one night my parents were to go to a wedding. Our regular babysitter was not available and there was a young local man who offered to babysit us. I knew there was something "off" about this young man, and I told my father I didn't want him to be our babysitter. My father knew enough to trust that I had good reasons and declined the young man's offer. Later we did find out some pretty unsavory things about this young man.

When I was around eleven, my father owned three or four cleaning stores, where I'd go to visit him at different times. At one of them he had a nineteen-year-old girl, Nancy, who I really liked and loved to just hang out with. There was a guy named Ted who lived on the second floor of the building and I'd often see him when I was hanging with Nancy. One day I went to see Nancy and she wasn't at the store. But Ted was there and he invited me to come upstairs to wait for Nancy at his place. I got an uneasy vibe— my ESP kicking in—and I said no, thanks. Ted tried to persuade me, saying he had things upstairs he wanted to show me, but I still said no. A short time later, my father showed up and said that Nancy wasn't coming in that day, and he took me away with him. Some time after that, I'd been in that store a few times and noticed that I never saw Ted anymore. I asked my father, "Where's Ted?" My earlier vibe not to go alone with him to his apartment had been correct. There was something terribly wrong with Ted. He was tormented. My father told me he'd been found in his apartment, dead. He'd hung himself.

The children of these new generations are waking up to the universe. They're using their love and kindness, and to a greater degree than generations before they are remembering where they came from. Children have always had the ability to see the Dead, but now as their parents are beginning to be more open about it, they ask more questions. They sense more acceptance of their curiosity on the subject, and they approach it as they would any other normal part of their world and their experience. Kids generally have a more highly developed sixth sense than adults. Isn't that strange? Actually, all of kids' senses are more sharply tuned than ours are, but we don't think of it that way because what we older people have that they lack is the means to communicate what we see, hear, feel, etc. So basically as we get older, our communication skills improve while everything else declines. What a system! But back to what I was saying, take the example of a child being involved in an accident where both his parents are killed. Only a five-year-old boy survives the crash. A crowd gathers around the wreck. Out of all the people present, that child will always gravitate to the individual who will keep him safe. It's built in. Even in a situation where some bad person wants the child to go with them, the child *knows* this person is not right. But generally, kids are taught by their parents that adults are authority figures, so they don't feel right saying no. They'll go against their own ESP unless parents teach their children to listen to those feelings and obey them.

Can children also actually communicate with spirits?

I do try hard not to overgeneralize, but I believe that most if not all children have this ability. But again, it has to do with how much support the child receives when they mention their experiences to parents or older siblings—others they see as role models. Some kids may get teased about their "secret" or "invisible" friends and so will keep quiet about who they see or speak with. And it is overwhelmingly the case that kids eventually shift their focus exclusively to what we think of as the material world and then will lose their ability to have these kinds of contact. Personally, the stories my clients tell me about children talking with their deceased relatives are some of my most favorite.

For one, there was a young woman who came to see me and told me that her mother had died a few years earlier and she was not ready to lose her mom. She was very sad and upset, just missing her so much. She had a daughter of her own who was just tiny when her mom passed. About two years later, she still hadn't completely gotten over the loss of her mom. One day her little girl (who was about four or five years old then) said to her, "Don't be sad! She's right here! She's going like this!" and the little girl puckered up her lips like she was about to give a big sloppy kiss to someone. Well, my client was completely taken aback. She told me that some years before, when her daughter was just an infant, her mother had told her about a dream she'd had. She'd said that she'd been dreaming about her new granddaughter and dreamed that she was kissing her. She woke up the next morning with her lips still in a pucker. She and her mom had laughed about that dream all the time while her mom was still living.

Another story that I thought was really neat was from a woman whose mother's brother (her uncle) was named Nick. Nick died when this woman was thirteen years old. Years later she'd married and had a little baby boy who she decided to name for her uncle. When her baby was around eighteen months old, she and her mother were visiting in her kitchen while baby Nick was upstairs in his crib. They could hear him on the baby monitor and were amused to hear him chattering away and laughing. Together they went upstairs to the nursery and little Nick was standing up in his crib. Joining in her son's high enthusiasm, she came up to him and said excitedly, "Hi! Who are you talking to?" And her son pointed across the room and said, "Nick!"

How can we use whatever level of psychic ability we have for the greatest good?

We all have a variety of psychic talents, which are all gifts from God. It's up to the individual to nurture and cultivate their gifts by heart and spirit, not ego. They'll manifest for the greatest good when the person who has the gifts submits to fellowship with God on some level and agrees to follow instructions from God to "deliver the goods." More and more are doing this, consciously. The veil that separates us from the Other Side is a dense consciousness. By the choices we make and the actions we take and the skills we develop, humanity is getting closer to Heaven—it's not Heaven getting closer to us.

What type of meditation do you practice?

In 1977, when I was twenty-four, I took a course in TM—transcendental meditation. This was back when I was trying to reconnect with the Other Side. As a teen I hadn't wanted anything to do with my ability; hearing from dead people was not something that every sixteen-year-old did, and I'd just wanted to be as normal as possible and fit in with my friends. But in my early twenties I was reconsidering, so this was one of the steps I took—learning how to quiet down and focus inward. For me, a very social, fun-loving type, it was very weird, but it really was good for me; it got me in touch with all I know about the Other Side. Basically, you can do meditation any way that floats your boat, whatever gets you to your happy place. Some might get there by saying a rosary or other prayers. You can put on low music, light candles, and sit back and think about all you love in your life. I like to take seven strong, deep breaths, all the while saying, "I'm turning it all over to you, God." I think to myself, "This is how I'd like my life to be," and then I mentally turn it over to God. It's always different. I love to do it just before I go to sleep. In many ways, my meditation is just my own prayer about what I would like to have, how I'd like my life to be—my work, the people I love. I can do it anywhere—no lotus position or meditation cushion required. I could be floating on a raft or driving with John or on my own and just be saying this kind of a prayer quietly in my mind. I tend to keep things simple—that's what works for me. Every now and then, maybe if something big is going on, I'll make more of a big deal about it, more of a ritual, or maybe sometimes I just feel like being a little fancier. But most of the time, it's just like any other part of my day, like making dinner—a lot of times you just don't want to fuss. Paper napkins are fine for the mac and cheese. Sometimes you have someone over; you go to a little more trouble—get out the napkin rings and linen napkins, candles, the good plates. Make a little more effort, make it a little more special.

Why aren't we all born pretty?

Keep in mind that in God's eyes we are all beautiful! And once again, it's a choice: Beauty can be how we see ourselves. What society calls "beautiful" or "pretty" changes from year to year, let alone from century to century. If *Project Runway* was set in the fourteenth century we'd see Botticelli cherubs on the catwalk, not six-foot-tall, eighty-pound sticks, but full legs, big butts, round tummies, big boobs, and small boobs. Physical beauty and our ideas about what is beautiful are transient but the spirit is not. God created everyone's spirit beautiful.

You believe that we keep our same personalities on the Other Side. What about someone who has brain damage, whose personality has been either stunted or vastly altered?

A lot of people will confuse behavior with personality. They really are two different things. So it's not really that the personality has been altered by the physical brain being damaged—whether it is congenital or from an accident or illness. At the soul level, the personality is the same, but the physical problem is inhibiting the person's ability to express their true nature. I admit that the effect—regardless of the reason—seems the same. But it's really not the same thing at all. On the Other Side, all is perfection, so the personality there is the true personality. Nobody brings brain damage to the Other Side. Since most people on this side do not have this kind of impairment, it's completely obvious that the personality is retained. In cases of physical brain damage on this side, again, we might see glimmers of the true personality, but the individual's physical limitations may keep them from showing who they really are.

Is it possible for someone who is not a psychic to see angels?

Yes, I do believe that under the right circumstances we can; the angels will show themselves to us, although we might not even be aware that what (or who) we are seeing is an angel because they may show themselves in a form that looks completely human. Someone who steps in and does a good turn for you when you are really in need and then "magically" disappears might actually be an angel. I had a letter from a woman who said that ever since her father had been diagnosed with Alzheimer's he claims to see angels. For a while he seemed to be frightened of them, but later he began to take his sightings in stride, waving to them and saying, "We see you." She said her mother was concerned, but she herself felt that it was possible his brain had been altered in such a way that he had a greater capacity for perception; in other words, he could see what was invisible to others. I would agree.

Alzheimer's and other kinds of dementia can be so frightening; it's so disorienting to not be able to make sense of things we used to take for granted. Sometimes the afflicted person is completely unaware, but other times, they are somewhat aware and it can be very distressing to them. In the case of this woman's father, instead of losing a capability, he's actually gained an ability—to see physically what usually is not visible to our eyes. Of course this can be scary, too, but it sounds like he has become adjusted and is no longer intimidated. He sees that they are not there to hurt him. We usually have trouble with things we can't feel or touch, but angels—if we could see them—are around us all the time. There's no reason to fear them.

Can ghosts travel, or do they only appear wherever they lived? For example, if my grandfather has never been to Spain, could he go as a ghost?

Ghosts, or spirits, if you prefer, can travel anywhere they please. The tendency is for them to hang around near loved ones, but these days, many of us have loved ones all over the world, not like the old days with six generations of extended family all together in a three-village radius. But to be clear, while generally speaking there is no place the spirit of our loved one would rather be than close by us, if they choose to go elsewhere, they can. This is God's gift to us when we cross over—the existence of our choosing. My father used to love to go for long car rides when he was here. Later in his life, his body wouldn't allow him that pleasure—he couldn't sit that long without pain, and he needed too many bathroom breaks to make it enjoyable. But once he crossed, I heard from him that he and my brother Harold were taking long drives through the mountains. That's what he loved so that's what he does. Somebody else could say, "Hey, I never had any time or money to travel when I was in material form, so I think I'll just zip over and see the Eiffel Tower," or "I always wanted to see a whale in its natural habitat," and they could do that. Anything that spirits are inclined to do or see, they can. Why? Because it's perfect.

If they were so inclined, could a spirit give us a hug?

Yes, I'm sure they can—at least they would be able to approximate the sensation of a hug. I did talk about this in my first book—how dead guys will sometimes mess with my feet when I'm in bed. This is done with energy rather than actual hands or body. They can energetically press up against you in bed or, yes, when you are in the shower. I've had people tell me that a dead loved one would sit on their bed and they could feel the depression in the mattress. I got a letter from a woman who said that a deceased loved one even tucks the covers around her sometimes. Another woman wrote to me that a few months after her husband had crossed he came to her during the night and pulled her close to him. Their dog was sleeping at the end of the bed, and at the same time she felt her husband, the dog began to whimper. Clearly both she and her pet felt her husband's energy. Another woman wrote me that one day she was cleaning in the bedroom when she noticed something out of the corner of her eye. When she turned, clear as day she saw a little boy who looked exactly like her youngest daughter. She knew the boy was her daughter's twin, who she'd lost early in her pregnancy. She was very comforted to know that he was still around her and, she said, knowing of his presence explained the occasional tugging at the lower back of her shirt she sometimes felt!

How can a spirit tuck us in when they don't have any hands?

It's all energy. I can't explain the exact mechanics of it, but virtually anything that happens here happens because of energy—from a seed growing into a plant, to cooking our dinner. We may stir a pot of gravy to help it along, but in terms of manual manipulations we don't have anything to do with making a plant grow. It pushes up out of the ground on its own. Spirits themselves are energy and somehow they manage to turn on the faucet in the bathtub, which to me seems like quite a challenge to do without hands, but they manage. We have to remember that our core essence is energy—our spirit form—and the body is just a shell or a vehicle. We're used to thinking of it as necessary but it's actually limiting; without it we are actually more powerful than with it.

What is the most important lesson you've learned from the Other Side?

It's hard to pick one, but this is the first that comes to mind at this moment. I'll just say a word or two (maybe several) about self-confidence. I consider myself a very confident person. I am not sure that I was like this since birth, but for most of my life I have been, and it's not just because I'm a big ham. I was fortunate to have loving parents who always supported and encouraged me. That is an incomparable blessing and it's one that I've thanked God for over and over throughout my life. I've also had the benefit of lots of help from the Other Side. Even though I was dyslexic and was not the best student in school, the Other Side always reminded me that I was a good person, I was worthy; they reminded me of the things I was good at so I didn't tend to dwell on the things that I wasn't good at the way some people do. It's like that TV commercial where the girl calls her dad to tell him she got an A on her advanced physics test and instead of being happy for her and congratulating her and saying how proud he is, he starts berating her for calling on the cell phone and using precious, expensive minutes to deliver her news. I know it's meant to be funny, but I'm sure glad my parents weren't like that! That's the kind of thing that can kill your self-confidence, make you feel like you can never do anything right, never be good enough, and that feeling or belief will completely ruin your life. Why does this matter? Because self-confidence is literally the key to having everything you want. The secret is that God wants you to have a life full of everything you enjoy—health, wealth, happiness, pleasure, love, and peace. Nothing left out. But when we don't feel confident, we don't feel deserving. When we don't feel deserving, we begin to self-censor. We say, "I shouldn't have that," or "I won't take that," or "Someone else probably needs that more." I'm not talking about being greedy or insensitive or ungenerous; I'm talking about taking yourself out of line anytime there is something appealing on offer, whether it's a career advancement, an interesting person, or a nice apartment. You know what I'm talking about. If it's a third giant slice of chocolate cake, maybe you *shouldn't* take it. But if it's a chance at wedded bliss, a vacation to Hawaii just for being the one millionth customer through the door, or a bow for a job well done, then take it! What's the harm? Use your judgment, people!

Some of the least confident people get in the way of their own greater happiness by pretending they are *over*confident. If you are one of those people who prides themselves on being a hard case or a tough cookie, then try flipping that switch. What do you get out of that, anyway? Is anyone really scared of you? And if they are, is that really a good thing? We all need each other. Making themselves seem unapproachable is the same thing as taking themselves out of the goody line. It seems to me that people like that lose more than they get, and in most cases, they started playing that role just so others wouldn't see that they were nervous or afraid about something themselves. So, like I said, why not try flipping the switch, try not being so tough, practice your smile repertoire, offer someone some help with a project or a tight spot they are in and see what happens. I bet you discover that you really are a strong, confident person without the tough-guy act. And instead of it being "I'm in control so don't you try to mess with me," it'll be "I'm in control and can make very cool things happen for you and me." Wow! Much better!

This is something I wish everyone would practice every day—telling yourself that you are perfect and good and happy. If you don't have someone in your life who will give you strokes just for being you and all the nice things you do (be honest—you *know* you do nice things), then you need to give them to yourself.

And last, let your self-confidence ooze throughout every aspect of your life, including how you view yourself physically—that's an area where just about everyone beats themselves up to some degree because they don't match a photo of some fifteen-year-old dolled up to look thirty in a magazine. Personally, I always look my best! That's just my attitude. Maybe you've seen this joke that goes around on the Internet from time to time. It's a picture of a woman looking into a full-length mirror, we see her from behind—she's got a butt a yard wide. But the image in the mirror is this beautiful shapely vixen. I'm telling you—*that's my mirror!*

When we are self-confident, the universe opens its arms to us!

You said it was hard to choose, so what is another great lesson you've learned from the Other Side?

Another lesson, which I think is equally important, is to respect one another, try to keep in sight the things that are really important, don't let small stuff make you nuts. All of this comes under the heading of making the effort to get along with one another.

As a spiritual reminder, John has a wall plaque that he is extremely attached to that has the words to the famous poem "Desiderata," written by Max Ehrmann in the 1920s. (Ehrmann was a philosopher and poet from Indiana. If you've never seen his poem, Google it—it's easy to find on the Internet.) "Desiderata" means "something desired as essential" in Latin, which I understand as an ideal of absolute importance. The poem begins, "Go placidly amid the noise and the haste/and remember what peace there may be in silence." It's all about a philosophy of being a loving person, acting with consideration and grace, and being happy and at peace with yourself. John loves this poem and wherever we have lived, he's insisted that it hang on the wall in our bedroom. And I have to say, in most ways, John really lives his life by this message. It's something that we both have had to work on. One time, some years ago, we were having an argument. Well, to be honest, that's putting it mildly. We were fighting. John walked out to go to work and I was on the phone complaining about him, when suddenly I heard a tremendous crash coming from the bedroom. I ran to see what had made the noise and there was John's plaque on the floor. With no one anywhere near it, it had fallen right off the wall. I didn't need anyone to explain the point to me—it was definitely the spirits reminding me of the importance of this poem's message.

On another occasion, another argument (how many times have I said it? I'm not perfect!), John and I were bickering, and our wedding invitation, which we have framed in a glass and metal frame, fell right off the wall. Again, not a soul anywhere near it. Even though it hit hard enough to get our attention, I was grateful that the Other Side felt it could make its point without breaking the glass.

Immediately when I think about these things, the importance of getting along and treating one another kindly, my mother-in-law and her family come to mind. I joke about them now, but I want to be clear, I really did try, for years and years, to do my best to make those relationships work. Finally, I had to walk away. All the Other Side asks of us is that we do our best. Sometimes a situation really is impossible. Sometimes in order to be your best self, you do need to separate from a person or a situation that is making you unhappy or keeping you from being your best self. Nobody on the Other Side expects us to stay in an abusive situation. Even if it's family.

Is there any way I can find out who my guardian angel is?

The only way I know to do this is to be able to tune in to the Other Side and see who is there. For instance, I know that my father and brother are guardians to me, but prior to their passing, I already had other guardians. Bear in mind, even if you were able to have the names of your angels, you likely wouldn't recognize most of them. These are spirits who have been with you through many lifetimes but this time around agreed to stay over there to watch over you while you had your earthly adventure. So in terms of your present life, you would not even remember them. When family and friends who you *do* know cross over, they join forces with these angels so your team gets even stronger.

Do we have more than one guardian angel?

In the vast majority of cases, yes. Most people have several or even many guardian angels. In only two cases in my entire career was I unable to make contact with anyone on the Other Side who was looking after an individual here. Why this should be the case, that these two people had no guardians, I honestly can't say, though I've struggled with the answer over the years. I think it's possible that, for some karmic reason, these two people were deliberately given no assistance this time. Like, "If you don't know how to swim, you better figure it out, or you're going down." Maybe they failed to assist when it was their turn so this lifetime is to balance that, or maybe they themselves opted to go it alone to achieve some particular lesson. It is also possible, I realize, that they actually did have an angel or two, but for some reason, their angel was not allowed to speak to me. I've wondered and wondered about this—from all different angles—but I don't really know what the answer is.

If my loved one has died before my child is born will they know about the new baby?

They certainly will. They often will participate in and see to the baby's send-off, wishing that soul good luck, and promising protection from their side of the veil. Often the child will have an ongoing connection with a family member on the Other Side for the first few years of his or her life, until (as usually happens) the child begins to focus more and more on the physical side of things, and loses this connection to spirit. This past spring I was in Chicago taping material to be shown to television producers, and one of the crew, a young woman named Tracy, told me the story of how her sister Donna had crossed before any of her own children had been born. Her children had never known their aunt. Yet one day, her young son, who was about three years old, woke up from his nap, saying aloud, "Happy Birthday, Donna." It was indeed her sister's birthday! She had known it and had been thinking about her sister, but had not mentioned the date to anyone. Clearly her son was enjoying a connection with his aunt, who he'd never met in the flesh.

Do unborn children come again to the same mother?

No, I don't believe they do. Not in the same lifetime. The unborn child and that mother will come across one another again; they'll know each other again. But I don't believe, from my understanding of the way things work, that that child will come again, as a baby, to that mother. That soul (the baby) had a particular mission for this particular life, to teach a particular lesson. Next lifetime, it's something different, for both the woman and the baby—and bear in mind that the "baby" may actually, in soul terms, be older than the "mother." Regardless of why the child came here but was not born, the mother will know the answers to this when she gets to the Other Side. There is a connection, a love bond, between these souls.

Are Down syndrome kids
highly evolved beings?

Absolutely, yes. I believe these precious ones chose to come here in this highly distinctive and very powerful form. I feel like before, this was less well understood, but as we all are becoming somewhat more enlightened, we can see what a gift these individuals bring. Whereas in earlier times these individuals would often be hidden away by their families, now it is not uncommon to encounter someone with Down syndrome, and they stir a significant feeling in our soul. We might mistake the feeling for pity, but it's not that at all. It's deeper than that. It's like a recognition of nobility. It's like they have come here saying, "I will change the lives of two people" or even fifty people, or more. There is a resonance and a ripple effect. When we encounter someone who has a tougher struggle like this, it rings a bell deep in our soul. It opens up an opportunity for us to learn and practice kindness and courage.

Does psychic ability in families usually skip a generation the way they say twins tend to do?

No, there is absolutely no rule about this. All cases are different, completely individual. God doesn't give you this kind of sign to look for. God sends what He wants to send, when He wants to send it. No formula to it. My grandfather was very psychic and he told my father that I was, too. But nobody clued us in that Bobbi Concetta, my brother Bobby's little girl, also would be. In our family, it skipped one generation between my grandfather and me, but it didn't skip the next one between me and my brother's daughter. Another thing to remember is that like other abilities, psychic ability is on a spectrum—it's not like you either have it or don't have it at all. We all have a bit; some have a lot. I'd be willing to bet there are a lot of people walking around with no idea how much they have, simply because they've never paid attention to it, or call it something else, like they have lots of "hunches."

So many people feel like when they die they are leaving important things undone or leaving a big mess for others to clean up. Are we really messing up? Or is this part of some plan?

Well, I'm not going to tell you to just let it all go and not to worry about it because that is just plain inconsiderate. If we care about our partners and our kids, or whoever we know will have the big job of wrapping up after us, we really owe it to them to have this in order as best we can. We don't always get to plan when we'll be leaving, of course, so common sense would say we should keep on top of our affairs as we go. But that would be a perfect world, right? And there's no such thing as perfection on this side. My answer to this question is that I do think that everything is part of the plan, even the unpleasant tasks that seem to belong to other people. Our karma is all bound up in our relationships and this area is no exception. The old saying goes, "You can't take it with you," and that goes not only for material things, but also our troubles and our secrets. So whatever kind of life we've been living, it'll all be revealed once we go.

Believe me, I've heard every kind of thing on this subject, from kids having to clean out barn-loads of saved stuff because their parent was either a pack rat or exceptionally frugal, to a spouse discovering hidden tax problems, to finding out about a second family—including wife and illegitimate children. Finding seven-teen lawnmowers that your dad meant to fix one day may bring a smile, even though it's a hassle to get rid of them, but finding out you may lose your home because your spouse had devastating financial problems you never knew about, or discovering kin you never knew you had, is a whole 'nother ball of wax. Yet all of them are karmic. They say something about the individual who has passed on, but they also put to the living person the question: Now, what are you going to do with this? They may feel shock, sadness, confusion, anger, or betrayal. They may want to take it off their plate, say it has nothing to do with them. But the fact is that while they are here, still among the living, they get to choose. How will they choose to behave? What will they choose to do? How will they choose to feel? Their initial response may be that they've been blindsided and they don't feel in control of their feelings. But once they absorb whatever new reality they find themselves in, they really do choose how they feel about it and deal with it—and they should know that they will receive help when they need it from the Other Side, very possibly even from the one who left them the challenge in the first place. Our deceased loved ones won't do all the work to bail us out of a situation here; they just aren't allowed to "fix" everything for us. But when we are doing our very best to cope and overcome difficulties, they've got our back. Meanwhile, while you are still here, it's up to you how you want to behave and be remembered—as someone who was trustworthy and open even when things weren't perfect, or someone who maybe cheated or hid things or was so fearful they couldn't be honest. That's what karma is all about. So yes, even the messes are part of the plan—the lesson plan.

There are so many different religious beliefs—does it matter at all what we believe?

It really doesn't. What matters is that we respect one another and try to love one another. This sounds like the simplest of platitudes, but it is the greatest single challenge we have.

Recently a husband and wife came to see me and the wife's grandmother came through. She kept telling me that everything was the same and showing me a cross. It took me a few tries describing what she was saying and doing before this couple "got it." Apparently, one of them was Greek Orthodox and I can't recall what the other one was, but something different. The grandmother had been very upset when they got married because she did not approve of them being different religions. It went against everything she had learned in her church and she had been really worried for them. They understood her message was that on the Other Side, all religion is one. Love is love and God is God and it's all the same. They did not hold the same strong beliefs as the grandmother, obviously, but it made them very happy to hear from her that this is what she'd learned after she crossed, and that she'd wanted them to know that she'd been wrong and everything was okay now, in her book.

So much of the violence and killing and wars throughout history have been "my God versus your God." Nothing has ever been won by this. Nothing. And nothing ever will be. Giving God a different name does not change anything except the way you are referring to Him. He is one. He's not sitting up on a throne somewhere saying "I'm more powerful than your God." There isn't another one.

Why does the energy of God exist at all?

It just does. It's just truth. Physicists can tell you the why of everything else in the world—from why the ocean is blue to why there's a sun in the sky. But no one can say the why of God. God just is.

What is our soul's purpose?

Generally, our soul's purpose is to learn how to become more God-like. (What makes each of us individual is our unique way of doing this—the spin we put on the ball.) Becoming God-like is everybody's destiny, but as in everything else, we have a choice. The gift from God is that each of us can become as joyous, successful, and satisfied as we choose. God gave us the power; we have the right. You might ask, but *how* we become more God-like? Just substitute the word "love" for the word "God" and use that as your guide. When you choose love you choose God, and when you make a loving choice you are more God-like than when you make an unloving choice. With every choice you make, choose love. In any conflict or challenge, ask, "What would love do in this situation?" The loving resolution is the God-like resolution. Becoming God-like is a tall order. We shouldn't be hard on ourselves if it doesn't happen overnight. We need to realize it takes time to learn our lessons. We can't be in a great hurry.

Is there any secret to getting to Heaven?

On the Other Side, a perfect paradise waits for each of us, so long as we don't deliberately take a life while we are here. The big secret is that we can have a near-paradise of our own making while we are here. I say near-paradise because nothing on this side will ever be perfection. On this side of the veil, it's all about the choices we make. The law of the universe is that what we send out is what comes back. People who send out positive energy will see good things coming back to them. But it's not like a yo-yo—throw it out and it comes immediately back in. Sometimes we have to be a little patient because the good thing coming to us requires a certain timing. There can be the same lag time with seeing the results of negativity, too, so people who are sending out negative energy often take a long time to realize it. When it comes back to them, they may not even connect negative things that are happening to them with the negative things they've done. They might even wonder why terrible things are happening to them. From what I have been shown, and also from things I've read, I believe that all negativity in the world is distorted and improper thinking, which leads to distorted and improper actions. God has given His full power to every one of us. What we do with it is our free will. We can make our lives a near-paradise or a living hell. Always keep in mind that God does not think evil is a good thing. You don't get any prizes for that.

Does everyone have past lives?

Yes, everyone has past lives; some of us have been back more often than others. This has to do with whatever our unique soul's purpose is, and also our free will, when we are on the Other Side, to choose to come back again. Glimmers of your past lives may show up in your personality, for example, how "deep" a person you are. You can have a wonderful sense of humor, but also have a lot of wisdom and a deep understanding and compassion for others if you've lived numerous lifetimes and have absorbed many lessons. You won't even be aware of why you know certain things; you think, "That's just how I am," but this is the reason. A person who acts out a lot and has little regard for others may just be a baby in soul terms—a very young soul with not very many lessons under her or his belt.

Past lives might also be indicated if you feel a strong connection with a certain place—especially if you've never been to that place in this lifetime. Maybe it's somewhere you've always wanted to visit, and if you do go there, you may even recognize parts of the place or get a strong sense of déjà vu. This actually happened to me. The first time I ever traveled to Europe was in 1999, when I made a visit to France. But some years earlier, I think it was all the way back in the 1980s, when I knew nothing about Europe, I "saw" myself walking down an old cobblestone street. I was out of my body and I was so consumed with knowing that I wasn't dreaming. The houses I saw were of an unfamiliar kind. I was walking, and I turned down a very narrow street. It was claustrophobic and filthy. I was thinking to myself: "Where am I? Do I know where I am?" Having the whole conversation, I even answered: "Yes. I *live* here." I turned into a doorway.

Years later in 2007, here I was in Rothenburg, Germany (also called Rothenburg ob der Tauber, as it overlooks the Tauber River). We took the famous—and truly fabulous—night watchman's tour, and lo and behold, I found myself on that very same street! Walking with John, I saw it just as it had been in my vision—though now much cleaner. Knowing I had once lived here, I was naturally curious to learn more about this place. It was a medieval walled city (thirty-foot stone walls surround the oldest, original part of the city), and during the Holy Roman Empire it was one of the twenty largest cities, with a population just under 6000 within its walls. Much of the town is still intact when nearly everything around it was leveled during the Second World War and rebuilt. The story of why Rothenburg survived is really interesting. During the war, the city was occupied by Nazi forces. The day before Easter 1945, nearly 40 percent of the old town was destroyed in air raids. But then the U.S. Assistant Secretary of War, John J. McCloy, got into the act. The story we were told was that McCloy's parents had honeymooned in Rothenburg. They'd shown him photos of their honeymoon so he'd always known about the town, its beauty and historical importance. Circumstances of fate being what they often are, it was this young man who was to give the order to destroy the city. He couldn't bear to destroy this place his parents remembered so fondly as where their marriage began, so he took it upon himself to instruct the U.S. Army General Jacob Devers to offer the Nazi command a chance to surrender rather than have the walls destroyed around them with artillery fire. While the German general rejected the offer, the local commander decided to accept,

and the historic buildings were saved. To this day, John J. Mc-
Cloy is remembered as Honorable Protectorate of Rothenburg.

From the website of the German embassy I learned another
fascinating fact about Rothenburg, which we didn't hear while we
were there: Its Christmas market (called the *Reiterlesmarkt*—there
is the most incredible Christmas store there!) was named "after a
local Teutonic legend, which began during pre-Christian times as
the story of a horrid rider who carried the souls of the Dead. As
Christianity swept through Europe, the figure developed from a
wild man into a loving, gentle man who gave gifts to all people
on earth." That's the kind of change I appreciate—anything negative that becomes a positive is A-okay in my book.

We all have our memories—they're all part of our soul. My
own soul drifts back from time to time, and I know that what I'm
seeing a small sliver of is a memory of a past life, not a dream.

How can we know about our past lives, who we were before?

Most of us have not had past lives as the Queen of the Nile or Rudy Valentino. And unfortunately, I was born just a little too soon to claim that I was once Marilyn Monroe. Most of us were and will be, lifetime to lifetime, "ordinary people." I put that in quotes because, what, after all, is *ordinary* about being born and living a human life? Each life simply explodes with potential—we can accomplish pretty much anything we put mind and material effort to. Each life is a miracle. Who were we before? I can only say what I've said before—look for the clues. What do you resonate with? A type of architecture or furniture from a particular period? A way of dressing? Are you drawn to the popular culture of a certain period (music, for instance)? Or movies or literature set at a particular time? What do you dream about? Do you have memories that don't seem to be your own—at least not from this present life? There are a good number of books that have been written by or about people who have had very strong experiences like this. Just one example is Jenny Cockell, a woman living in England who kept having disturbing recurring dreams about her own death. (Her book is called *Across Time and Death*.) In her dreams, she was very upset but she knew it was not because she was dying. Over the course of months and years, her dreams eventually provided more details and led her to discover that she had been a mother in Ireland, leaving ten children when she died, with an unreliable husband. She'd known that her children would be split up after she was gone and so could not die in peace. Likely it was this strong worry for her children that made her wish to reincarnate so soon after she had died. She eventually was able to go to Ireland, discover the setting of all her dreams, find all her children, and reunite them. An amazing story—yet, this is the reality of each of us—we cross to the Other Side, and in due time, we come back again.

Do children have better recall of past lives than adults?

I've certainly noticed this—and I'm far from the first to say it; there have been whole studies done on this phenomenon. Children frequently will know quite a bit about their past lives. They are still connected to another time or place. There have even been cases where a kid will speak a foreign language that he never heard in his family, at least not this lifetime. One time a woman came to see me and she told me that her family had just celebrated her little granddaughter's fourth birthday. The child was blowing out the candles and the grandmother had said to her, joking, "Just remember, I'm always going to be older than you!" The little girl gave her a look and said, "But the *last* time, I was older than you!" There was just something about the way she'd said it and the way she'd looked at her grandmother that this woman knew that she was referring to another life they'd shared together. She told me, "I felt bad because I knew she wanted me to say, 'I remember.'"

In their younger years children still are somehow connected and still remember this stuff. It could be something really small, like remembering a little piece of their old daily routine, or something special that made an impression on them then. For instance, a woman who has come to see me a couple of times has a little seven-year-old boy. When he was about five or six years old, she told me, she and her husband were taking him to see the movie *Bambi*. On the way, the boy began talking about the movie, what he remembered about it. My client and her husband were puzzled and amused. "What are you talking about?" his father asked him. "You've never seen this movie before." But the boy persisted and really seemed to know some details of the film, which surprised his parents, and they weren't sure how he could have known so much about the movie. "How'd you know about that, when you've never seen it before?" they asked him. "But I did see it," he said. "It was when I lived in that big green house and my name was Walter!" He'd seen *Bambi* last time he was here.

Once we evolve and no longer come back to Earth, what is our purpose?

At that point, we are a spirit master; we are leaders, reporting directly to God, and at the same time are one with God, like the right hand reporting to the head. However, just because we are no longer required to reincarnate for lessons, it doesn't mean we *can't* come back to earth. A spirit master might choose to return—it would be what we think of as a sacrifice—in order to fulfill some higher good at a particular point in time.

Why do we have certain people in our lives?

We come in touch with those who for destiny purposes are in our lives to support us and to help us grow.

Sometimes we meet people who we might feel have no reason to love us. We're not really related, we might have completely different backgrounds, but there's a connection there. There's something about them that we just adore, something that is enriching to us, something you just can't put your finger on. They love us, and we love them back. I don't have children of my own, but there are some people in my life now who are just as dear to me as if they were my very own child. My son-in-law is not part of my biological family. He's married to John's daughter. But he is very dear to me, like my own son. And I know he feels the same. He wrote the most amazing poem for me, framed and everything, about how he feels about me. It is such a special present, and I totally love him for that and for just who he is.

There is no such thing as just friends. Anyone you are friends with has a long-standing connection with you over many lifetimes. But there are also people who don't even really touch our family circle but whose presence in our lives is meaningful and supportive. You may have known them in another life, but on the periphery. Let's say you lived on the same street for twenty-five years, and you always got your bread from the same bakery, week in, week out. Whenever there's a wedding you get your cake there, and when there's a funeral in the family, the people who own the bakery send a box of cookies with their condolences. They aren't family, they aren't even really friends in the closest sense, but they are a pillar of your neighborhood, people you see over a period of time, familiar, friendly, caring. Next lifetime, will you be married to one of them? Probably not. But they might be on your bowling team—cheering for your strikes, groaning at your gutter balls, sharing a beer. We forget about these relationships, and they are extremely important, very therapeutic in ways we never really stop to consider. Every single one of these individuals is in our life for a reason.

Does this mean we have a spiritual relationship with everyone in the Astrodome or Giants Stadium if we go to watch a game?

No, no more than rooting for the same team, though I know for some that is a spiritual experience. I'm talking about people who you interact with over a period of time. Your bowling team, people you compete with, eat and drink with, joke and commiserate and bitch with—that's different from someone you just happen to sit next to. If you have season tickets and actually form a relationship with the person next to you over the course of a season or years, that's different. That easily could make them part of this extended soul group I'm talking about. But not every kid selling peanuts, pennants, and programs will be spiritually related to you.

If spirits reincarnate, how can we retain a single identity and relate to a single set of loved ones—living and dead—and have a single set of likes and dislikes?

When we reincarnate, we tend to do so in soul groups. I don't mean that a whole bunch of souls get off the cosmic bus together like a high school baseball team showing up at an away game. I mean that in a somewhat staggered way (over generations—child, parent, grandparent, etc.) these souls will come to this side having long-existing connections with one another. The relationships will differ. Consider that your family, friends, and close acquaintances are being reshuffled, repurposed, recycled. Maybe that's a crass way of putting it, but that's the main idea. One time you are the child, another time you are the dad. Next time you're not actually in the family, but your friendship is so close you seem like a family member. So it's not like, if you've had sixteen or sixty different lifetimes, you'll have that many individual sets of loved ones. For the most part, they will be the same spirits—each of us working with and helping those in our soul group to learn to love, grow, and evolve. For our own part, Shakespeare said it well: "All the world's a stage, and all the men and women merely players." Basically he means that the individual is like an actor who comes to the world to play a role. Robert Downey Jr. may play the role of Charlie Chaplin and years later play the role of Iron Man. Each of these characters might have different characteristics and mannerisms that the actor has chosen to affect—whether consciously or unconsciously. But the core of the actor is the same basic soul. Just as it's said that our taste changes every seven years (so if you don't like broccoli as a child, try it again later in life), so, too, our ideas can change; our tastes can change in only one lifetime, let alone several. So certainly the soul will not be static in its likes and dislikes—nor should it be, if we really are making an effort to evolve! But certain things are likely to remain and to be a core characteristic of that particular soul.

You've said that we are all here to learn lessons. What if we get a failing grade on the test?

While we're still on this side, there are a lot of lessons we get to try over and over again. Not everything—sometimes we have just one chance in this lifetime to get it right—but in most cases there is a second chance, or even a third, fourth, and fifth chance. In many cases, too, getting it "right" is a subjective measure and might not mean as much as at least *trying* to get it right. In any case, nobody here gets to be the judge, even if they think they are. Since that includes me, I can't really say who's passing and who's failing. I can only have my own opinion about that. And, to the best of my ability (bearing in mind I'm human), I try only to have an opinion about whether *I'm* doing things right or not. In most things, I think I'm doing a pretty good job. But as much as I joke about it, and as much as I've become used to the fact that we don't get along, I'm really worried about the job I'm doing with my mother-in-law. I am aware that our relationship is karmic and that I've been presented with a challenge. There is a lesson for me there. I tend to joke that the lesson is that you can't please everyone, but sometimes I worry that this answer is too glib and there's something I'm missing. It really does worry me. And if I'm to be honest, it hurts me, and I wonder and worry if it also hurts her. Sometimes I feel like I've done all I can; sometimes I wonder if there's something more I can do. Why can't I get this straight? Whatever more may happen here, I know when I get to the Other Side, my questions will be answered, but I worry that I'll also have to come back and try again to learn this lesson properly. I personally can't answer the question of "what if," but I can suggest an approach to our lessons here, and that is to try to keep an awareness that the challenges we meet are lessons, to keep your eyes and ears and mind open for solutions that might be different than the first thing that comes naturally to your mind. Try to look beyond the easy answer. If the answers were easy, it wouldn't be much of a lesson—we'd all just be staying the same.

If my partner and I fight, does this mean we're not really soul mates?

Oh, brother! That is one of the biggest misconceptions of all time. It's such a fairy tale—we'll find our soul mate and live happily ever after! That's a real load of you-know-what. Let me say it once: Soul mates are still work. You still need to show up, be invested, pay attention, give a little, take a little (or sometimes give a lot, take a little). When we're on this side every relationship is first and foremost a human relationship, which is a messy proposition. It's working at our lessons, balancing our karma. It's not meant to be free from discord. I think a lot of people have the completely wrong idea about what a soul mate is—they think that you're standing in a crowded room, like at a party or in Grand Central Station or something and your eyes connect and there's a lightbulb that goes off, or sparklers, your ears pop, and you move in slow motion toward one another, run straight to the preacher or City Hall, get married, and live happily ever after. That's so crazy. First of all, soul mates might not even be lovers—they may be brother and sister, sister and sister, parent and child, or friends. Basically, they can be any combination of two people between whom there is a healthy, beautiful, harmonious flow that seems to come naturally. When we connect with our soul mate it's to take on some task that God wants us to get done. Often there's no romantic element to it, just deep feeling for one another, deep respect, and deep commitment to whatever the work is. Whether or not the pairing takes the form of what we think of as a romantic relationship, it could be rocky at the beginning, there may be karmic things to be worked out before they can get down to business, so to speak. It might even take years to discover the ease and harmony we associate with soul mates. My husband, John, is so perfect for me. But nobody would have known that from our first ten years. We were on the road to divorce every other week, mostly due to outside forces. We were constantly fighting over friction caused by other people. It took an unbelievably long time to rid ourselves of that negativity, and sometimes I don't know how we did manage to stay together and reach the profound happiness and joy in each other that we have now. Obviously the connection was very strong, even when it didn't seem that way. I might look at another relationship and see a lot of strife and think judgmentally, "No way are *they* soul mates!" But that's not fair—I have no way of knowing what the connection is, how deep and strong it is, what its purpose is, or what is required of this pair before they find an even keel. Another thing is, I think a lot of people overdramatize the soul mate thing. In some ways it's really like the English would say, "That's my mate," like "my best buddy." It's that kind of closeness. The tendency to overdramatize who and what a soul mate is is what causes disappointment or might make someone think they don't have a soul mate or haven't met their soul mate.

So the romantic idea of a soul mate isn't real?

To be honest, usually not. There is, from time to time, the type of magical tale that we commonly associate with soul mates, though. When one of my clients was only eleven years old he was visiting his cousin who lived in another town. There he met a little girl a few years younger than him—she was only about eight. His cousin introduced the two of them and they were joking around like "how do you do," and they shook hands. When he touched the little girl's hand he literally got an electrical shock. When he was twenty-two, he met a girl. She seemed familiar to him. They talked for a while and realized they'd met before when they were children, that she was the little girl who had given him such a shock when he shook her hand. He told me he'd never forgotten that experience and knew in his soul that this connection, the shock, and their meeting again, was no coincidence, that there was something about her that was familiar to him at the core of his soul. They've now been married for thirty-five years.

Why is it that some families are really close and others hardly seem connected at all?

All families are karmic. We've all been here before and we come here again together for each soul to have a karmic life lesson. There may be an orderly answer to this question, but if there is, I haven't been told. It seems to be individual. A family can seem close, but one significant event—a death, an illness, a betrayal, even something "accidental"—can completely rip that family apart. Some families, everyone is spread out all over the planet, kids all living in different towns, or even different countries, but still, they all show up for holidays or rally when there is a family crisis. In my own family, on my mother's side, she and her two brothers were put in an orphanage when she was just five. She was on the girls' side, her brothers on the boys' side, separate. When they all got out, they stayed in touch. They married, and stayed married to their spouses to the end of their lives. They lived in different states yet they made the effort to keep in contact, called each other, visited. Who knows, karmically, why they had to go through what they did, having to live through such horrific childhoods in a terrible orphanage? But whatever the reason, it didn't pull them apart; they stayed close in spirit even when they were far away from each other and got together when they could. Another family, they might all live right around the corner from each other but don't even want to speak to each other. They might hold grudges for small disagreements and practically make up reasons not to speak. The kids will avoid their cousins' weddings. Then some of them will be puzzled why no one wants to get together for the holidays. Well, you can't have it both ways. You have to invest in the relationship if you want that warm, fuzzy feeling on special days. You can't turn family off and on and expect it to resemble the fantasy. You need to stay engaged or there is no healing. I don't mean to suggest that this is easy, or in some cases even doable. I definitely know of cases where someone has had to leave home and have no contact with their family of birth in order to find peace and healing for themselves. Maybe there really is nothing that can be done in this lifetime, or maybe they will reunite later and be able to do their healing then. But one party wasn't ready for or up to the required challenge, and the other had to give themselves space from a situation that may have been toxic or dangerous. This is an interim solution—in some cases, even a necessity—but I believe that at some point they will have to try again.

Why do tragedies seem to run in some families—like all the men dying young, or multi-generational alcoholism, or mental illness?

All families are soul-link groups. Before coming here, they have individually chosen to come back together to try to learn particular lessons or overcome challenges of many lifetimes. To be clear, I don't just mean what is obvious to us here and now: that this family has been troubled through several generations. I mean lifetimes that may be separated by decades or centuries. We're all familiar with the buddy system. Since grade school, when you went on any kind of outing, the teacher would pair you up, you held hands, and you and your buddy looked out for one another, kept each other from getting lost or separated from the group. In the adult world we're familiar with various self-help groups, from Alcoholics Anonymous to diet clubs, where two people will be partnered up to keep an eye on each other or to be there to call if their partner is feeling tempted by alcohol or the chocolate cake they are trying to get out of their life. In a sense, the soul-link group of such families ideally acts like "buddies" to one another. They have a deep understanding of what the other (family) members of their group are going through. They live it themselves; it's their shared personal context, even if some are stronger and some are weaker. But they all came here with memories of past wounds and weaknesses. Together, this lifetime, they have the chance to take their power back, heal their issues. They can work together as a team. If they accept God's love and let it guide them, they can overcome.

What are some of the causes of "family karma"?

As I've said so often before, our karma is individual and probably not simple. When you are dealing with several souls there may be things between the individuals as well as things that all together are trying to learn or heal. In one twenty-four-hour period, we do and say so many things that either may heal karma or create more karma, so you can just imagine what may have built up over several lifetimes. If we apply a little common sense to our spirituality, I think we have a better shot at healing our karma—family karma, or any other kind. The word "sorry" is a very good tool, for starters. That one word, if it's offered sincerely, shows a willingness to change. I've personally spent a lifetime looking for answers, looking for healing, looking for a way to make each new day better. And I'm nobody special in this regard. It's pretty much the same game for each and every one of us. For the whole darn family!

The idea that we come here with karma should be empowering and freeing rather than daunting. For example, I have an old friend who for many years suffered from depression. She was in therapy to try to get to the root of it. She went back week after week to talk about all the negative things that had happened in her life. There was no one major thing, just a number of smaller things that seemed to have piled up. She couldn't seem to let go of them and just get on with her life. It wasn't until she was introduced to the concept of karma, the fact that, never mind what had happened to her in *this* life, the reasons for her sadness might be rooted in other lives that she had no conscious knowledge of, that she was able to quit gnawing the bone, so to speak, and dedicate herself to finding and creating and spreading happiness in *this* life. That's all any of us can do. We can't change past lives; we can't undo karma. We can only do the best we are able to in this life, balance our karma or burn it off. Knowing that is very powerful.

What's going to happen in 2012?

So much has been written about the year 2012—how everything will be turned upside-down or even obliterated. Supposedly this is predicted by the Mayan calendar and even, some say, by a secret hidden code in the Bible. There are even some who believe the Earth will be struck by an asteroid, or that aliens will come and either wipe out the human race or colonize the planet. The notion that this year will be completely different from those leading up to it and following it is not really true. We're not going to be singing "Auld Lang Syne" at midnight, wishing each other a Happy New Year, and then BOOM! The lights go out. Or maybe the lights come on. The changes that are attributed to 2012 are already in progress.

God doesn't wear a watch—the changes are happening all around us. The question of 2012 is about a shift in consciousness: spiritual transformation. It's an opportunity that we all are being given, regardless of race or religion—or lack of religion—to connect to God-consciousness within ourselves. It's a chance to say YES to this invitation. It's so important because if we say yes, we—humanity—will come, more and more, to rely on love to resolve our problems instead of force or control or violence. I don't believe that the world is ending. While it's not one of the top questions, I've been asked about this a number of times. For instance, one woman wrote to me on my MySpace page saying that she was afraid to have another baby because she already had a child and felt that even with this child she wouldn't have enough time to be with him if the world was going to end in 2012, so if she had another baby, it would only be a toddler, and then they'd all disappear or something. I honestly don't mean to make fun of someone's fears—we all have something we are afraid of. But some people like to dwell on the negative. (Please understand, I'm not saying this is the case with the woman who wrote to me; I'm just trying to make a point.) They're *full* of fears—to them, any change is scary. People don't realize that we are changing all the time and some changes are for the good! The time surrounding 2012 (and as I said, events that are prophesied are already going on now—things that are global don't happen overnight) has the potential to see some amazing changes, but the change won't be dramatic unless we all take God up on the invitation to bring more love into our lives and use love as our primary means of relating to one another. The news doesn't focus on positive things, but there is good happening all the time. We're becoming more responsible to each other and to the planet; there are lots of beautiful stories that aren't being told.

I guess here's what I would say to anyone who's still worrying about the world coming to an end in 2012: Don't worry so much. You can't spend your life this way! You want to know what's gonna happen or where you'll be in 2012? *Plan* something. Put it on your calendar—a trip to Disney World or Italy, as you prefer. Put your change in a jar and label the jar 2012. That's for your trip. If anybody tries to worry you about "everyone's all going to hell in a handcart when the clock strikes 2012," you tell 'em, "*You* can go wherever you want. *I'm* going to Italy."

What exactly is it that animals do for us?

The best way I can say it is that it seems that animals carry God's love to us. There are all different kinds of animals. I'm not sure that different animals bring different aspects of God's love or if maybe it's just that each of us recognizes and relates to a different kind of animal and that's God's way of getting His love through to us in a way we'll be accepting of it. Maybe think of it as product packaging—a different package appeals to a different person. Some people (very few, thankfully) will say they don't like animals, but then a stray kitten or injured squirrel finds its way into their heart in spite of themselves. Some of us don't distinguish—we love every kind of animal, whether furry, feathered, or finned. (We might not like all the bugs, but we try!) Every now and then I have a bad night when I'm not able to sleep; maybe I go to bed upset or worried. One particular night I felt completely stressed, just tossing and turning. My brother Harold came to me and took me to a beautiful pond with baby ducks and puppies running and tumbling around it. He told me, "You can play with them, you can hold them." It was just so calming. Not just calming, but really joyful. I was so relaxed and happy. It's true that animals are a gift from God—they can change our whole attitude, spending time with them can heal us. The funny thing is that even when we think we are helping them, we are really helping ourselves. If we try to save a bird that has broken its wing, we are giving our care and attention, but the feeling that we get from that might be a sense of self-worth. If we try to calm our big baby of a dog who trembles at the sound of thunder, we're being given the opportunity to practice compassion. Different creatures bring different gifts, but ultimately all the good stuff is just different forms of God's love.

Isn't there any such thing as a bad animal?

Really, there isn't. Every animal is from God. Every creature is here for a reason. Sometimes an animal could be in our way or scare us, but that doesn't change the fact. We have a lot of bears around our home in the woods of New Jersey. This past spring, John was out working in the garden and I happened to look out the kitchen window and saw a bear right behind him. I banged on the window and managed to get John's attention and he was able to get the air horn (we should call it the bear horn since it's kept just for this purpose) out of the garage and scare it off. Just a short time after that, after a bookstore signing event, I got a note from a woman who'd attended. She said, "You told me I should be careful on the way home, and as I was driving along a bear came out in front of my car! Good thing I was paying extra attention!" I'm glad the bear didn't eat John, and I'm glad this lovely woman didn't hit the bear, but if either of those things had happened, it wouldn't make it a bad bear. They're both just bears being bears.

Can a dog that has crossed over reincarnate as a cat?

This is a new one for me, and I'm not really the pet psychic, so bear in mind that this is my best guess based upon my own observations, stories I've heard, and things I've read. I'd say, yes, I believe this is possible. The Egyptians held that no person could be reborn as an animal (and I know this is true; our souls are different—the energy of animals' spirits is a different frequency from the energy of humans' spirits), but they never said that an animal could not come back as another animal. There are certain dogs that behave very much like cats—aloof, persnickety, always looking for a soft pillow to curl up on. Just as one example in the other direction, a friend of mine was telling me about her friend's cat, who will bring a ball to its owner when it wants to play fetch. This cat will literally retrieve the ball over and over. It loves this game as much as any dog, but that's pretty weird behavior for a cat. Is this a common occurrence? It doesn't seem to be, but as I said, I don't consider myself the expert here. There are other cases you may be familiar with— the giant tortoise that "mothered" an orphaned baby hippo after the tsunami in Indonesia, or the crow befriending the kitten (there's a cute video I've seen on YouTube). Are these examples of animals who have reincarnated with a "remembrance" of being a different species? Or are animals evolving, too, and are these stand-out examples of ones who have learned enough love not to be ruled by their traditional, instinctual fears, to be able to befriend and help others that are not of their kind? Stay tuned! These are great questions, which I hope to learn more about myself.

Can pets see ghosts?

Absolutely, they can. Haven't you ever seen a dog that is just lying peacefully on the floor and all of a sudden, for no reason (or at least no reason you can see) the dog jumps up like it's had its tail pulled or something and runs out of the room? Or haven't you ever seen a pet—dog or cat or whatever—look like it's looking at something that you can't see? You try to get yourself into the same sight-line to look at whatever they're looking at and there just isn't anything there? They definitely are catching something that you ain't getting! They may not see them all the time, even though spirits are with us all the time. But it's not at all unusual for an animal to see a ghost.

I used to have a gray and black tabby cat that John and I rescued from a welding yard. Actually, there were two kittens, but we found a home for her sister and just kept the one. We named her Lucia, but one day we came into the living room while she was lying regally on the sofa and John said, "Look at her—looking like Madame Foo-Foo," just something he made up, but it fit— she had so much attitude, she was looking like "I'm all that and a bag of chips." It's funny how those things go—you always think you've got the perfect name for your pet but end up calling her something else. From that day on we always called her Madame Foo, or just Foo, or sometimes Foofy. In any case, Foo had the run of the house, she could go anywhere she liked, but never would she venture into my office where I hold my appointments. It was just uncanny how she would avoid that area, clearly because of the spirit activity there. Frequently it happens that if I'm to do a reading for someone the next day, the spirits who want to connect with that person know this and will gather at my home the day or the night before! But they usually hang right around my office area. I'd always feel bad for Foofy just before I'd go do one of my big shows in Verona—lots of people, more than your average gathering of ghosts—and not staying in their usual area. Poor thing used to freak out. She could not find a place anywhere in the house that was a ghost-free zone! Really, that poor girl didn't know what she was getting into when she came to live with John and me.

Can our pets come back from the Other Side? And if so, what would be the reason for this kind of visit?

Oh, it's very common for a pet that has crossed to come back to visit "their person." And it can be for many reasons. It might just be to comfort that person, to keep them company. It might be almost out of habit—pets often form very strong attachments to us just as we do to them. A pet might come back and make itself known in some way to try to remind us of something— even if they just want to remind us of *them*, and the love they had and still have for us. My friend Page, a writer in Manhattan, told me how on the one-year anniversary of her cat Barney's passing, she found paw prints on her white living room windowsill, as if a cat had walked in through her window from outdoors. Mind you, Page's apartment is on the third floor of her building and this was not a window that had a fire escape or any way for an animal to climb up to that window. As Page told me, "I may not be the best housekeeper, but there's no way I could have had paw prints on my windowsill and not see them for a year!" She knew that her dear little cat had come to pay her a visit and she was very moved by this.

Do our pets reincarnate, like humans do?

God's got a lot of secrets and that's not one I've been given the answer to, but I can tell you that I have heard some stories that lead me to believe that at the very least, our pets can act somewhat like our guardian angels and human spirits on the Other Side, in that they have a hand in sending a new friend our way. Sometimes they have enough of a connection to us that they are able to let us know what's going on, when a new pet is coming so we can keep our eyes open.

After my first book came out, I was at the Rockaway Mall and I went into Book World. I always liked to stop in whatever bookstore I'm near and be sure they have it—I'm so proud of it. I saw a guy who worked there and I started to ask, "Do you have *Do Dead People* . . . ?" He says, "Stop right there—we just got a shipment in. I'm just opening the box." I told him, "Oh, that's okay, I wasn't looking for it, I just wanted to be sure you had it—that's my book!" He says, "Oh, my god, you are, like, the most famous person in Boonton!" That cracked me up. But I'll take it—it might be a small pond, but I'm the big fish! Anyway, we got to chatting a bit and I told him that for the book I was working on, I planned to put in a lot of stories about pets because so many people asked me this kind of question. He said, "Really? Well, I gotta tell you about my cat. My cat was more than just a pet; she was everything to me. But when she was eighteen years old, she got sick and I had to make the very hard decision to have her put down.

I just felt terrible about it, but I couldn't stand to have her suffer. It was just the kindest thing to do, even if it killed me. That night I had a dream that my cat was sitting at the end of my bed. The dream was so real, and in it my cat told me, 'In six months I'm coming back.' She said, 'I'll be all black, and I'll be with my brother.'" Well, six months go by and this gentleman is watching his calendar and he knows it's time for his cat to return to him if this dream is at all true. So what does he do? He begins checking out all the shelters in the area, one after the other. He told me he literally went to ten different shelters, looking for an all black cat with a brother. Finally, in the last shelter, he finds a pair of cats that fit the description, just like his cat had described to him in his dream—a brother and sister, the sister all black. She needed surgery for a hernia, so nobody wanted to adopt them and take on that expense. Well, he did, and the cats have been with him ever since.

Another amazing story: My friend Barbara is a monkey—that is, according to the Chinese zodiac. She's also part wood nymph (not to mention, she's more psychic than most). She lives in Queens, very close to Alley Pond Park, which is mostly woods, and for many years has loved nothing better than taking her dogs for walks along the trails there. Barbara has only one human child, her daughter, but she's had lots of furry-faced, four-legged children, and that's really how she feels about them. Where another person might have framed photos of their family, Barbara has framed her favorite pictures of her beloved dogs. When one of her pets crosses over, for her it's just as crushing as losing a child. A good number of years ago, Barbara had a little mixed terrier with big, brown eyes named Penelope who looked a lot like Dorothy's Toto. Penelope was a bossy little dog, but well-behaved and a sweetheart. One day in March—March 23, to be exact—when Penelope was eight, Barbara's daughter was talking with friends in the street in front of their home, and she inadvertently made a motion with her arm, which Penelope understood as "Come." Sadly, a car was coming and Penelope was hit, and later that night died at the vet's office. Barbara was just devastated. She decided she could never have another dog because she just couldn't bear to replace her dear "child." For ten years, she lived without taking in another pet. Then one night, she had a super-vivid dream. In it, she saw Penelope, who was telling her that it was all right for her to get another dog. She was so moved by the dream that the very next day, which "happened" to be March 23 and Easter Sunday, she put Penelope's photo in the breast pocket of her blouse, right over her heart, and she and her daughter went to the North Shore Animal League shelter. (She told me that at that time North Shore used to go around to other shelters and take the animals who had outstayed their welcome, the ones who had not been adopted and so were scheduled to be destroyed, so many of the animals there were on their "last chance.") Amazingly, it was open on Easter Sunday, but given Barbara's usual family holiday gathering, they only got there in the evening and it was near closing time. Still, they were shown the animals and as they walked, cage to cage, room to room, her daughter would say, "What about that one, Mom? Don't you think that one is cute?" But Barbara just wasn't feeling it and kept saying no. Finally they get to the last room—as they walked in, there were cages directly ahead of them, and to the left and right. But suddenly Barbara felt an intense burning on her upper back, right between her shoulder blades, like her back was on fire. It was so intense and strange that she turned to see what might be causing it, and noticed more cages behind her that she hadn't seen before. Her eyes were drawn immediately to a cage on the top shelf and she saw a dog completely identical to her Penelope—except that this dog was male and had amber eyes. Without even asking a single question about the dog (how old is he? is he in good health?), Barbara walked up to this dog and said, "Do you want to go home with me?" The dog's lips quivered like he was trying to talk to her, and his eyes communicated, "Yes!" Barbara wasn't even surprised to learn that this dog, which she named Zachary, had been brought in from another shelter only hours before Barbara and her daughter arrived. On the way home, poor Zachary threw up in the car, but Barbara didn't care. She said to her daughter, "Just you watch! When we get home, this dog is going to walk right in and act like he's lived there all his life." And from her lips to God's ears, that's exactly what he did!

Do pets have karma like humans do?

Basically, karma is the process of balancing our negative and positive actions from lifetime to lifetime. We are spiritually "held responsible" for our actions since we have the gift of free will. For the most part, the choices we make are not life or death choices. Sometimes they are, but for the most part they are preferences—we'd rather do this than that. No matter how sneaky you think your own dog or cat is, animals can't intellectualize about whether a behavior is good or bad, right or wrong. They are simply acting on instinct. Does a cat have a karmic debt for killing a mouse? No. Does a dog have karma to balance if it chews up your favorite shoes? It might seem to us like it *should*, but again, no. If a guy gets eaten by a bear, it is because of the *guy's* karma that that happened. The bear doesn't get karma for eating the guy. The only karma our pets have is the karma of unconditional love. The only karma animals in general have is being a gift from God. Just don't ask me how getting eaten is a gift!

Does an animal have the same kind of soul a person does?

Truly there is something more to this question than what has been written other places, but I do think it's a mystery that we won't get the answer to until we get to the Other Side. There is something so special about this gift of animals to us; they are a real soul connection to God. But I just don't know specifically what the situation is in regard to the animal's soul itself. Still, it's so obvious to anyone who has, for example, a seeing eye dog, or anyone whose pet has alerted them to the smell of gas in their home, or anyone whose pet has come up to them and licked their face in a consoling way when they are going through a divorce. There's so much love being given. All throughout history we have stories of how someone was injured and some animal went through hell and high water to get them the help they need—way before Timmy and Lassie! God only knows what this connection is. As unsatisfying as this answer is, I just want to say, simply, it's a gift, and I think those who understand this are truly blessed.

This is a story one of my clients told me: For years, she had had two cats, brothers, but they didn't look anything alike. One was small and solid black; the other one, named Echo, was an oversized tabby. Because he was so big compared to his brother, she used to tease him—fondly, of course—and call him Double Cat. The smaller brother had passed away three months earlier when one morning around 5 AM, before the sun was even up, she heard Echo making an unusual noise that woke her up. Actually,

Echo was having a heart attack, and before she could do anything, he died. As you can imagine, she was really upset. The vet wasn't even open yet. She called and got the emergency number, but it was past the point when anything could help her cat, so instead she waited until the vet's business hours and took the body of her deceased pet to be taken care of. She went back home very sadly and lay down on her bed, crying and crying. Suddenly, she realized she was surrounded by an absolutely HUGE light. It got her attention and she stopped crying. In her mind's eye she saw very clearly the image of a huge, regal lion, which she knew instantly was Double Cat, and she heard the words: "This is who I've been all along." It was an amazing visitation. Her beloved pet was showing her his true divine nature, or soul, if you will—"This is who I've been all along"—and she knew that through all the gentle teasing, she had loved him, and that he knew it, and he really *looooooooved* her, with a lion-sized love, in return.

Is there any advice you can give for how one might comfort a child whose pet has crossed over?

For kids, losing a pet is often like a dress rehearsal for losing a human loved one. It's our first time with the experience of not being able to hold on to someone or something we love and who has given us joy and comfort. Even for an adult the loss of a pet can be traumatic, let alone for a child. Whether a pet has been hit by a car or simply died of old age, you can tell a child that God has asked that this pet come home so that He can give it the care that it needs. Tell the child that if he or she asks God to give them a beautiful dream about their pet who has crossed over, He will:

Are animals psychic?

Probably both psychic and telepathic. Animals are very in tune with us and with each other. And I think we all, maybe even to a greater degree than we are with each other, are in tune with them in return. This is probably because we don't feel threatened by our pets, so we are more open to them and with them. It's so true it's a cliché that our pets (especially dogs—cats can be a little persnickety) give us unconditional love.

I have to say, I'm pretty good at tuning in to people, but nobody beats my very best friend Mushy for tuning in to animals. Mushy (aka Cornelia) and I have been friends since we were nine years old, and I can tell you she is the pet psychic of all time! She is just amazing with animals—growling dogs treat her like the Queen of Sheba—and nothing is more important to her than a creature's well-being. I recall one time we were visiting Mushy's mother at Marco Island in Florida. We were on the beach and Mushy saw a seagull stuck in the sand. Its wing was broken. Mushy swung into action—she ran up the beach and got a box from a concession stand, put her towel in the box, and laid the bird in it so gently. We'd never been to the area before, but that didn't stop Mushy— she found out where there was a vet and we drove there. She told them, "I don't care what it costs. If you can fix it, fix it. If you can't fix it, you need to put it down. I don't want it to suffer anymore!"

For a pet, Mushy's preference was always for dogs. She had a pair of Siberian huskies—Beau, a male, who we called Bowsy, who she'd bought as a puppy, and a female, Nicky, who she'd rescued after her third home. It had been a real nightmare for poor Nicky. Mushy had found her chained in the basement of some loser's house. She'd been completely abused. Nicky never really got over it and was always a little gun-shy. But Mushy took her in, gave her a ton of love, and the two huskies were her big buddies until they both eventually crossed over. At different times over the years before, I'd said to her, "Mush, why don't you get a cat?" but she always said, "Nah, I'm really more of a dog person." Well, lo and behold, right after her second dog passed away, these two feral cats showed up in her yard like they knew there was a heart open for the taking. But for a long time, they kept their distance. Slowly, slowly, she won them over and got their confidence, and to make a long story short, this pair, Red—a male—and Precious (aka Mookie)—a female—ended up the new pets-in-residence. Red since has crossed over from cancer, but Precious has been with Mushy for over ten years now. It was uncanny. Somehow these cats just knew. It was like a call went out in the wild: *Cornelia D'Nunzio has an opening!* and you didn't have to tell them twice.

One of my clients who lives in a small apartment building in New York City shared with me a story that really is a great illustration of cats who just "know." One of her cats had cancer—she was doing all she could for him, but there was a limit to the care she could give. The bottom line was that her cat was dying, so she was just trying to make him as comfortable as possible while he was still on this side. For months he would always be curled up on a pillow, next to her own, on her bed. The building she lived in was near Central Park and there were a lot of animal lovers living there, lots of cats and dogs, and during the time her cat was sick, before he crossed over, it seemed like every cat in her building somehow got loose or "ran away from home" and ended up at her door—at least six cats—which is a little much for a coincidence (and you know what I think of coincidences anyway). She was constantly scooping up cats and returning them to their own apartments. It was like they had come to pay their last respects to her dying cat. Somehow they were all connected; they *knew* what their four-legged neighbor was going through.

Do all good pets go to Heaven?

All. Pets. Period. Go to Heaven. That's *ALL* pets. That includes the ones that growl or hiss or spit at you, the cat that clawed up the sofa, the puppy that chewed up your favorite flip-flops, and even the "mean" dog that bit you on the ankle. Animals aren't born mean or bad. They all come to us as gifts from God. If someone starves or mistreats an animal, well, animals will react as if something like that was done to a person. They'll become fearful or angry or depressed and will act out in various ways, whether it's cowering or crying or fighting back. They'll even run away from those who would offer real love to them because they are so used to being abused that they'll mistrust even loving gestures. Sometimes when you adopt a pet from a shelter or whatever, it can take a long time to win the animal's trust, depending on what it went through before you took it into your life.

A gentleman named Eric sent me an e-mail asking the question in this way: "Being that animals are also creations of the Creator, I would imagine that they are also spirits. So once my existence on this plane ends, will I be able to meet animals that I have met that I considered to be great friends while I lived on Earth?" I just love the way he phrased his question. Animals are indeed our great friends! What I can tell you for certain is, the energy that was your pet has been created by God and cannot be destroyed. What frequency it is communicating on, I honestly don't know—I haven't quite mastered the interspecies thing. When I am doing a reading, I'm not hearing from the animal directly. What I do hear, over and over, is the spirits telling me that the pet is there. Oftentimes they'll give me a name—this is really challenging because we give our pets the craziest names, so it's not like I'm trying to understand a name like Mike or Jane. It's stuff like Babaloo or Muggins or I don't know what! Sometimes the spirit will tell me something the pet used to do while it was here, or tell me something special about the relationship, so I can communicate that to my client. But never have I had a client ask me about a particular pet and had the spirits say to me, "Nope. That was one bad dog. He didn't make it through." Even that dog that you never could quite housebreak will get to go to Heaven, the one that no matter how good he tried to be was always having accidents—the kitchen floor, the living room rug, the guest room carpet. One thing I say over and over is that there are no accidents. That goes double for the Other Side, and in this case I think that's something we can be very glad of!

What is the most difficult thing about being psychic?

For the most part, I really love my life. When I was younger I was very concerned about fitting in, not wanting to be different from other kids my age, the usual teenage/young adult concerns. But now I'm used to being who and what I am, and I realize how blessed I am to be able to do what I do and to be able to share a sense of hope and peace with so many people just because of the work that I do. So I don't feel I have much to complain about in that category. But one thing that isn't always comfortable is that I'm so super-sensitive to emotions. I can't stand being around negative energy. It's really hurtful to me at a soul level. I don't want to make anyone paranoid, but I'm really very perceptive of how someone really feels about me when I meet them. An example of this that actually can still make me feel a little wistful or sad is that when I was a little girl I just loved *The Andy Griffith Show*. I thought Opie was the luckiest boy to have Andy for a dad, even though, of course, I adored my own father completely. But he just seemed so nice and kind. He always managed to solve all the funny problems everyone around him created. Well, one day when I was around eleven years old, my class went on a field trip to Newark Airport. I have no idea what he was doing in Newark, but some of us spotted Andy Griffith, who looked like he'd just gotten off a plane. I was so excited to see the star of my favorite show, naturally I thought this was my big chance to get his autograph. I ran up to him and said, "Are you Andy Griffith?!" and with the greatest contempt and impatience he snapped, "I was an hour ago, kid." I could feel his energy so strongly—why he was so upset by a little girl trying to connect with him, I have no idea. Logically, I know it wasn't personal; maybe they lost his luggage or something. But his annoyance and disdain just penetrated me and really broke my heart.

I've learned over the years not to put myself into circumstances where the energy is going to be less than loving. But before I really learned this lesson, I worked at a place where the boss was a complete psychopath, a raving lunatic. He never communicated anything in a calm voice; he screamed at everyone. It was torture to work there, but it was a time in our lives when John and I really needed the money. Unfortunately, I'm so sensitive to energy that this guy didn't just give me a headache; it went to the very core of my soul and was making me sick. I was just beginning to heal from ten years of abuse from my husband's family, and working there was un-doing all of that. One day this guy got so psycho, screaming at me, that I knew I had to get away no matter what— he was literally killing my soul. The problem was, I couldn't quit; I had to get unemployment. So I told the office manager that he had to fire me or I was going to go and come back with a lawyer and file a lawsuit for the boss's abusive behavior. I'm not the idle-threat sort of girl and I guess the manager could tell that, so I knew I'd get action. I went home and I told John what I'd done and we put together our plan for the next day. The next day, I got up and went into the office real early, packed up all my stuff in six boxes. I was ready. A little later, I got called to the boss's office, and I was perfectly calm because I knew that the office manager had done whatever he needed to do to get me fired and out of there. I went in and stood there in front of the boss. His nostrils were flaring, his face was red, he was screaming at me, and I was just looking past him out the window, watching John's truck pulling up, just like we'd planned. I was practically humming a little tune inside my head. He finally got to the point of saying "You're fired!" and I had to really work not to explode laughing. I just said, "No problem, *Tom*." I headed back to my cubicle and he literally followed on my heels to be sure that none of my friends would dare to say goodbye to me or wish me luck or anything. Just as we got to my cubicle, there was John, who said, "Okay, hon, where's your stuff?" and then my boss—I mean my *ex*-boss, thank God—realized that I knew all along that I was going to be fired. He loved to hurt people, but this time he didn't get the glee of seeing me cry or even seeing me pack my stuff. All done! I was protected by the Other Side.

Do the Dead ever "give it a rest" and let you alone?

I don't have any beef with the Dead. If I want some peace, I can ask them, politely but firmly, to chill out and let me sleep or whatever I want to do, and they pretty much will be respectful of my wishes. To be very honest, I have more trouble with the living. There's hardly anywhere I can go where I won't be asked for a spontaneous reading or something of the sort. My appointment list is full a few years ahead of me, and if I let my assistant, Elena, open it up, I can't even imagine how much further into the future it would fill. But still I get calls and e-mails and am approached at every social gathering. I sincerely do sympathize with anyone who has lost a loved one and is desperate for news or to be consoled or given assurances straight from the horse's mouth, but I'm only one person. I've really got an appreciation for doctors and lawyers who I know are approached similarly, often by people they've just met, for a sampling of their advice. I mean, can you imagine? You're a doctor and you work long hard hours, and you go to a party and just want to sip your drink and laugh and relax like everyone else, and you've got people coming up to you saying, "I've got this stomach problem—a lot of green stuff coming out . . ." ? People really don't understand what it takes to do a reading. To them it looks like a simple conversation. But it takes a lot of physical energy; it's very draining. When I go to a party, I don't really want to be talking to dead guys. I'm there to *live* it up! I want to be talking about sex, drugs, and rock 'n' roll. I may not be *doing* those things, but I'd rather be *talking* about those things.

Is there never any time that the Dead bother you?

For the most part, no. Every now and then they may tease me or, if I'm not expecting to see one of them, I might get startled, but I'm pretty used to them. I guess if there was something they wanted me to do that I wasn't doing they might give me a hard time.

The Other Side played a huge role in John and me getting the house we are now in. They helped us find it and they helped us be able to buy it. They had big plans for this house. But it was before I went public, when I was still trying to decide whether I would or even could or not. And they weren't very happy with my ambivalence. They constantly would turn the lights on and off. And I'm not talking about just when we left the room. They'd do it with us in the room. And not just the lights but the TV. It used to make John completely insane that they'd do it right when he was in the middle of watching some program or game—the TV would just go off. For no reason. Well, no normal electrical reason, anyway. However, once I made the decision to go public, this activity completely stopped. Whereas before it was constant and random, now, only every once in a while there is something they do, and it's always in a friendly way, like when I went for a week to Mexico City and got back home, they gave me a bit of a light show—my assistant, Elena, and I kept having to turn lights out from room to room the day I got back. As soon as we'd walk away, they'd turn them back on. But it was more like a game, just to say "Welcome home." There's always activity, but I'm just used to it. And I also have an elaborate alarm system to alert me as to whether an "intruder" is in the flesh or on the spirit. So far, so good—just a lot of dead guys. I live with them and they live with me.

Since you have been psychic all your life, did you always know that you would write a book and be a public figure?

Not exactly. I had no idea that I'd be writing books, but I definitely had the "knowledge" that I'd somehow be the center of attention. To some degree, that's just my personality—also, I was voted class clown of my high school. But getting to this point was definitely a roundabout route. An incident stands out for me: In 1979 I was working as a receptionist in Clifton, New Jersey, for a fragrance and flavor company called Givaudan. To me it was just a job. I didn't have any particular love for what I was doing. Even though I wasn't doing much to *fulfill* my belief, I'd always believed that one day I'd be performing in front of huge crowds, so actually assumed I'd be an actress. That would certainly suit my personality better than answering the phone and making coffee. In any case, around this time, I'd met a new guy and I was going out a lot and staying out late and then getting in late to work pretty often, which, even as little as I thought about it, I knew wasn't endearing me to the bosses. In fact, I knew I was going to be fired. "They'd" confirmed it, and I even knew when it was "the" day. The way gossip was in that place, though, you really didn't need to be psychic to know. *Everybody* knew I was going to be fired. When I got called to HR, everyone was peeking out of their little cubbyholes as I went by like in *Dead Man Walking.* When I walked into the room I almost said, "Let me put you out of your misery, I'll just pack up my things." But then I thought, "Nah, let 'em have their moment," so I didn't say anything. I let them do their bit, which was exactly what I'd expected, and I headed back to my desk and got my things together. I don't know what compelled me—maybe the way everyone just kind of cowered in their offices, snickering, like "Oooooooh, Concetta didn't behave right and now she's getting the boot," like a bunch of scared little children—but just before I walked out the door I stopped and turned around and said, loud enough for all of them to hear: "Just so you know—you're gonna all be hearing about me one day. I'll say good-bye today but you'll be hearing about me again!" Ever the drama queen! I'm ready for my close-up now, Mr. DeMille!

I might get some of my drama from my father, Manny Ferrell. My dad really was amazing. There's a story I've heard more than once about when he and my mother were first married and they bought a dry-cleaners called 1-Hour Martinizing in Nutley, New Jersey. My dad was a real people person; he got along with practically everyone. But he had one customer who apparently decided to see if he couldn't work his last nerve. This guy had dropped off a pair of pants to be cleaned. When he picked them up, he opened the plastic to inspect the pants and he pointed to a spot that was still on the pants. He said, "The spot is still there. I'd like these done over." My father said, "Sure," and took the pants back. The next time the guy comes again to pick up the pants, he again opens the plastic and calls my father over and again points at this spot. He says, "I told you, I want this spot out!" My father, fairly calmly says, "Sir, not every spot will come out. This may well be one of those that won't." The guy says, "I want you to clean these again and I want you to get rid of the spot." So my father takes back the pants and cleans them a third time. The guy comes back in, takes his pants, opens the plastic, and blows up—"How many times do I have to tell you?? I want you to get rid of that spot!" My father calmly picks up a pair of tailor's shears, reaches for the pants, and cuts the spot right out of the pants. He says, just as calmly, "You want the spot out? It's out."

But I digress. Even being a psychic, I don't always know what the future holds for me. And even when I'm given hints, the specifics need to unfold in their own time. Unfortunately, time on the Other Side is a very different matter from time over here. Like everybody else, sometimes I just have to be patient.

If you could connect with any performer, who would it be?

I assume you mean one that has crossed over, but the sad fact is that I can only reach individual spirits with whom I have had a personal connection, either directly with them or through someone dear to them who is still here. And to tell you the truth, some of my favorites are still here. My favorite singers of all time are Judy Garland and Bette Midler—one on the Other Side, one on this side. To me, Judy Garland was the best *performer* of all time. At a time when performers were practically *owned*, she was never entertaining for the studio moguls. It was for the audience. That's what kept her alive. The audience was her IV bottle going straight into her veins. While I never saw her perform live, I'm still such a fan—seeing the movies, the clips of skits and songs—I so get it. I wish I could be like Judy Garland—I'd love to have her talent in any category, but make better decisions about my life. Of course, also Marilyn Monroe—count me among the millions. I'm a HUGE Marilyn Monroe fan. I have a zillion books, photographs, and also a zillion photographs of myself mimicking her. Call it corny or call it whatever you want, but I love to "play Marilyn." Any woman who wants to feel appealing or sexy can relate to Marilyn. And Bette Midler—I'm very glad she's still among us here. I love Bette Midler's singing and I love that she goes around New York City planting trees and starting neighborhood gardens and cleaning things up where the city has fallen apart and been trashed in years past. She spends so much of her life just trying to make things more beautiful. God bless her voice, and God bless her passion to clean up the world! So many entertainers are so endeared but they are protected by their "people," their publicists, and so forth. So many show themselves eventually to be not really a nice person. But here's Bette Midler out there with rubber gloves on, picking up garbage. That is humble and beautiful. Some stars talk a good game, but meanwhile they are living in gated communities, or on ranches somewhere, far from everyone. As if they aren't human, just like everyone else. Those are the ones who aren't in touch with reality. They really should get out more—the real world is not such a bad place!

Will our deceased loved ones be in close vigil with us before we ourselves cross to the Other Side?

Generally, yes, they will. And we often will be aware of their presence, will know who it is who is waiting. But there will be others that we aren't necessarily expecting who will be with the ones we *are* expecting. I've done many readings where the person who comes through tells me to tell my client that he or she will be there to lead them over to the Other Side, or there to welcome them when they get there. Nobody makes this trip alone, but just as we can't know all our guardian angels—some of them are people we've never met in this lifetime—we can't know our entire welcoming committee until we see them. Then, of course, we will recognize them as people we've known before, over multiple other lifetimes.

I got a letter from a woman named Sherri, who responded to my newsletter, where I'd said people could send any questions they had and I'd try to answer them. She told me that when her son was two years old, her grandfather died at the age of ninety-one. On a nice day, she and her son would walk to a baseball field that was just around the corner from her grandfather's old house. One day her son was waving and saying hello to no one. When she asked who he was waving to, he said that he was greeting "Baby Pop," which was her grandfather's nickname, and Jon, her cousin, who had died on 9/11, years before her son was born! After that, there were several occasions when her son mentioned seeing and talking with Baby Pop and Jon. He'd wave to them and tell his mother what they were wearing. Then one day, they were at the ball field again and Sherri asked her son if Baby Pop and Jon were there. He said no, and proceeded to tell her that Baby Pop had gone to "Dee Dee's house." (Dee Dee was what her son called her grandmother.) He said Baby Pop told him that he was going to Dee Dee's house because Dee Dee was tired. Two days later, her grandmother was diagnosed with third-stage cancer, which had already spread throughout her body. Her grandmother passed away two months later, and since then her son has not mentioned seeing Baby Pop or Jon. She asked me, did her grandfather and cousin come to get her grandmother? Of course the answer is yes, they did. The souls are always close by and never more so than when someone is about to cross. The one who is preparing to leave will be more aware of them, but even the rest of us are able to notice the vibe, too, at these times. It sounded from Sherri's letter that when her son reported his connection with his great-grandfather and cousin, she was welcoming, not fearful, which gave him the support to continue reporting his conversations with them. Hearing these messages from her son allowed her to have the comfort of knowing that her grandmother was well taken care of, surrounded by loved ones, when she crossed.

Have parents who experience the loss of a child angered God?

The answer is that this could not be further from the truth. I'm not sure why this question is asked so often—I've also been asked whether Satan has anything to do with it when a child dies. Perhaps because a parent who has lost a child so often feels like they themselves are in absolute hell. It's so tragic—I want to be careful how I say this—but God has a perfect plan. I assure you that a child who crosses, crosses to God, and the fact that they return to God at a young age has always been part of the plan. They knew when they came here that they would not be here long. When I meet a parent who has lost a child, it's so hard. I want to be a comfort, but it's so difficult to convince them that God is not angry with them; *whatever* the circumstances of the child's death, they need to forgive themselves. Even if there is a lesson for them in this situation, the question isn't, "Why would God do this to me?" The child came knowing they would leave at this time. Satan had nothing to do with it. Thinking that Satan had anything to do with it implies that Satan has power over God. Life, death, and everything in between is the business of ALL-mighty God.

Besides people who lose a child, there are also those who would do anything to have a child and yet they are not meant to be parents in that way. Again, this is all according to God's plan. It has to do with our individual karma and soul's purpose in this lifetime. I can use myself as an example in this case. I desperately wanted to have a child of my own. I tried everything—in vitro, fertility surgery, and many other things. But, I'm not God. This was not something I got to decide. I had even been told by the Other Side, when I was very young, that I would never have a child, but I fought against it. It took me a long time to completely accept that I had another purpose and to have peace in my heart on that account. Now, even though I didn't get what I wanted, I'm happy. There's no way I would sit around and be miserable and complain to God. I don't know everything that He knows. All I know is that there is a plan, *for each of us.*

How can a loving God let innocent children be born with terrible diseases or defects?

I think there's more than one question here or maybe it's just that the answer is connected to other things that don't have anything to do with birth defects or disease. First of all is the matter of how we define these things. We will call something a defect when what it is in reality is a sign of a particular challenge—or mission—that individual has. It's hard for us to understand this because we only relate it to ourselves. If we are reasonably perfect in our body, we've got all the usual parts and they all work in the way we expect them to, more or less, we think of this as normal. Then anything that differs from this model of normal, we call a defect—it isn't there, or it doesn't do what ours does. But what we don't realize is that, according to the greater plan, it isn't *supposed* to be there, or it isn't *supposed* to work in the same way. In our human terms, we often perceive suffering in that individual. In human terms, they do suffer. But these individuals are what are called "mission entities." They literally are here on a mission to have some powerful impact on us. They shock our emotions, they cause us to grow spiritually, at a faster rate. Mission entities are not always children, but it tends to be the children who we notice more, who tug at our heartstrings even more than if we would see an adult with the same challenge. The effect on us is more powerful. Not to make any kind of a joke about this, but in a very real way, they often become the "poster child" for a particular issue that we all need to solve. They pull our awareness to an ongoing tragic circumstance, where there has been much suffering for a long time, but we just aren't focused enough on it to work for a change—whether it's a cure for a particular disease, or to heal a sickness in society.

We also need to keep in mind that God's glory and the love He has for us is so great that we all are perfect on the Other Side and have no limitations, regardless of how we were here. A couple came to see me whose little boy had crossed over when he was just five years old. During the reading, their son came through and he said to me, "Be sure to tell my mother that I'm riding a bike!" He also said, "Tell her not to cry," but of course that was pretty much a lost cause. Tears flowing, the mother told me her son had had a disease that made his bones very fragile, so he couldn't play with other children because he was easily injured and wouldn't heal properly. She was always asking him what he wanted to do—did he want to watch a movie, play a board game, have something special to eat? He never wanted to do anything except watch other children. Any time she asked what he wanted to do, he wanted to go to the park. He couldn't walk, he had to be in a stroller, but they'd go and sit together and he'd watch the other children playing, and he'd laugh and giggle, getting so much enjoyment out of just watching. He especially loved to watch kids riding bikes. He was never sad; he was always trying to cheer up others. It just broke her heart that he couldn't play like the other children, only watch them; he would never be able to ride a bike himself, but he never complained. Her son actually lived longer than they'd been told to expect. Just before he died, she saw him looking toward the ceiling of his room, toward the corner of the ceiling, and he stretched out his arms like he was reaching toward someone. Then he turned to his mother and said, "Mommy, they say now I can do anything I want!" and then he crossed.

Why does God allow suffering?

I always say that it is this side of the veil that is the difficult side. The Other Side is perfection, but not here. In fact, this side is often called "the vale of tears." It's not only pain here, of course, it's a mixture of both joy and pain, but here is where we learn our lessons and grow spiritually. It's a Buddhist concept that everyone feels pain, but not everyone suffers. What this means is that we can choose how we accept the pain in our life; we can transform pain to something else rather than choosing to answer our pain with excessive grieving or depression. But I will admit that it can take years or even lifetimes of spiritual practice to fully grasp and embody this truth. That doesn't mean that we shouldn't start now.

My friend Barbara, whom I've spoken of before, is such an animal lover. She has a huge heart and can't pass by an animal in need. One summer day, she had gotten her couple of dogs on their leashes, heading to the woods for a walk. As she was passing a parking lot on her way, she saw there were a lot of birds perched on nearby buildings and, strangely, they all seem to be watching a particular car. Barbara walked over to the car and saw there was a tiny creature under it—very small with its eyes still closed. Without even looking at it closely (she told me she thought it was a mouse!) she put the animal in her pocket, turned the dogs around, and ran back home. Once there she set about getting a box, lining it with a piece of fur, looking for an eyedropper, heating milk to try to get the tiny animal to eat. She finally realized that it was a kitten and was *so* young, really just born. Her little terrier, Penelope, had taken a shine to the kitten and was avidly watching over it while she called her father to ask his advice. Her father was not very encouraging. He said, "Honey, there must be something wrong with it. It's really not common for a mother cat to just abandon a kitten like that unless it has something wrong." She hadn't noticed anything, but trusted her father, so she had another look at the kitten and saw that he was right. On the inside of one of the kitten's back legs was an open wound. She realized she'd need to take the kitten to the vet the next day, but for then she just concentrated on trying to get the little thing to take some of the milk she'd warmed for it. That night as she slept, Penelope came to her, barking to get her attention. She could tell that the dog's agitation had to do with the kitten, so she got up and followed her to the box she'd prepared. Immediately she realized that the kitten had died. Barbara was very upset. Even though she'd only had the kitten less than a day, she had completely bonded with it. She cried and said out loud to God, "I thought if You were giving it to me I'd get to keep it!" But clearly, this was not to be.

Exactly six months from the day she'd found the kitten, her birthday, Barbara was in a fairly serious car accident and was taken to the hospital. As she lay on a gurney in the hospital hallway, she spoke to God again, asking why He would have this happen to her, what lesson was she supposed to learn from this? Hadn't she been humble enough? Hadn't she shown her gratitude enough? What could possibly be the reason? She had more shocks coming.

Within the next three weeks, her father died. And then her beloved Penelope was hit by a car and also died. The losses were nearly unbearable, but for Barbara, an answer was forming: *Noth-*

ing was hers to keep. She realized that all she had, everything good in her life, was temporary, and only hers by the grace of God. She did not own anything. It was God's love for her that gave her all she had.

Into each life some rain will fall and we just need to do our best with whatever form that takes. God doesn't give us more than we can handle, even if it seems like it sometimes. On the material plane, nothing is permanent. Only on the spiritual plane are we eternal in God's love. This is the only true reality and it is all joy. Here, many of our lessons come with hard knocks, but we have to remember it's not intended as a punishment. We are confronted with our problems and our diseases to learn and grow. Princess Diana took off her gloves and kissed AIDS patients. This made her glorious! It's difficult for humans to comprehend this—we operate from such a narrow band of knowledge. It's up to us, to the best of our ability, to make the imperfect more perfect. To comfort one another when we are in pain, to learn, and to love.

Why do the Dead do subtle, not obvious things to get our attention? I've been trying to communicate with my mother and I'm not getting anything.

It's not *always* the case, but usually the Dead do choose to use subtle means, not big stuff. But be honest, if your mother gave you the choice, "Do you want me to show you the bird I used to love best, or would you prefer to have a piano dropped on your head?" how many of us would pick the piano? If you want to think of it another way, when we are here on earth, it's like we're in school, and what do they teach you at school? To pay attention and use your head and look for your answers. In *The Wizard of Oz*, Dorothy wasn't handed her answers—she needed to experience them. Nobody said, "Let's just cut to the chase, Dorothy. No point in making that journey when all you're gonna learn is that there's no place like home." She had to go and find out. It's the same for all of us. We need to experience; we need to learn and come to *know*. For example, your own little hometown is so nice, you have bingo nights, there are lots of civic events, etc. And what do you think? *Boring!* Then you spend some time away, and all the stuff that seemed quaint or not that exciting, now you remember how sweet it was just to be around family and friends and have a shared sense of belonging. You couldn't be told that; you had to learn it. Our loved ones, as much as they want to connect with us and comfort us, aren't going to wave a literal flag in our face. Your mother will allow you to use yourself, let you learn to rely on things beneath the surface. Keep your eyes open to look for small signs—pennies that always seem to turn up in your pathway as you go about your daily life, a butterfly that is hanging around your house on a special day. Keeping yourself open to seeing some sign and not ignoring the little things is the way to build a connection. You're not going to get a letter from your mother, some postcard with the news: I am here!

Have you ever tried to contact someone who already has been reincarnated? If so, what was the result?

This question came as a response to my newsletter from a gentleman named Patrick, and I have to say it is not a question I've been asked before, and I have to say that even though I immediately knew the answer I had a difficult time figuring out how to say it! But here goes: Since my communication is between here and the Other Side, if someone was already back over here, I would not be able to reach them. In that case, it would be like trying to telepathically communicate with someone I didn't even have any idea who or where in the world they were. The simple answer is actually twofold (but still simple, now that I've unraveled it). 1) I just would not be able to reach them. 2) This wouldn't happen. From everything I have been told, those we have known and loved who have crossed before us will all be waiting on the Other Side to meet us when we cross. The glory of God is such that He wants us to have the opportunity to all be together again. We don't reincarnate until all of those who belong together have reconnected, so there wouldn't be anyone here looking to find someone there who has already come back.

Can I ask my deceased mother to help me meet my soul mate?

Just to be really clear, again, a soul mate might not necessarily mean "husband" or "wife." That understood, sure you can. But you likely won't need your mother's help because that individual is either already in your life, or is destined to be at some point. If the latter, even with your mother's help, you might need to wait. But usually when I'm asked this question (or *one* similar), what is really meant is, can I get my mother's help finding me the right guy or gal—a mate, not a soul mate, who might even be their brother or sister in this lifetime. You definitely can ask the Other Side for help with this so long as you also are doing your part to be open and out there. It's not impossible, but it'd be pretty rare for that person to literally come knocking on your door (not ruling out the UPS guy), so give your poor deceased mother half a chance by going out and doing things you enjoy. Then, for goodness' sake, keep your eyes open—pay attention when that guy with the nice smile accidentally upsets your latte at the local Starbucks, or when that cute dog in the park has an interesting somebody at the other end of the leash. "Meeting cute" doesn't just happen in the movies!

How does my deceased mother know who the right person is for me? And how can I know that I'm getting her message right, that this is *the* one?

Your mother (or father, grandfather, nana, or whichever loved one you have on the Other Side) is with God and God has the Book of Life open in His lap. He wants to help you (just in case your mother doesn't—just kidding!). She and God are creating the calendar of events that bring your love to you. And here's something else to think about: If you know in your heart what a great catch you are, but can't find the right person, don't you think that there's a great person here who also has somebody on the Other Side who is looking to help them out? So really, you have two teams of angels working together to bring you and that special person together because it will be a beautiful thing for *both* of you! But you have to do the work, too. You have to trust and believe and be open. There is no case too tough for the Other Side when it comes to love. It's true: Some people aren't getting any sex in the city. But a lot of times that's because they aren't open to it. They're so sure it's hopeless, or sometimes their standards are all out of whack—they are imposing a standard on a potential mate that they themselves don't even meet.

I really am so lucky to have found John, and I really believe that the Other Side had something to do with putting us together. I don't know what he'd say about this, but from my side, he and

I are the perfect match. He's so calm and patient. He doesn't get upset about how much I talk—I talk so much it's like someone put a quarter in my back! And can you imagine if I was married to a funeral director or something like that? Yikes!

My mother used to say that for every pot there's a lid. In other words, no matter how much of an odd duck a person is, there is another person out there who will be the right fit for that person. But living life to this point, and running into some pretty strange folks, I'm not so sure there really *is* a lid for every pot. Some people may just have to use tin foil!

Is our time of death "etched in stone" before we get here, before we are born?

Yes, to a degree, it is. There's a basic plan. It depends on the particular soul's journey. Normally when and where a person leaves this side has to do with when they complete the job they came here to do. Whatever our job is, it just takes the time that it takes. When we go to the Other Side, it's a big homecoming party, so that's something to look forward to—eventually! However, even if the job isn't finished, if a person's body or mind becomes depleted, or if that person finds themselves in a situation where they are limited or stopped in their ability to grow, then they can choose to go. All is rooted in free will.

When I tell someone that the Other Side has told me something is going to happen—it could be a marriage, a birth, getting a new car or job—I'm never quite sure about the timing. Often I'll be given a clue, but it's nothing definite. They'll sometimes try to convey that it's right in front of us or right behind us, but they can't really tell me it's gonna be this Tuesday at 7:24 PM. At one of my recent big shows, I was doing a reading for a woman, and three brothers and her mother came through. I was a little shocked that she'd have three brothers on the Other Side already, since she didn't look that old to me. I knew they were trying to tell me something about time and I couldn't figure it out. I had just said to her, "They are telling me that you are in good health and will have a long life." She was a little surprised by that, but I guess I didn't notice right away because they were still talking and I said, "Are you seeing some particular time on your clock all the time? Are they maybe showing you a time to let you know they are around you? Because I'm getting something about time and I can't quite figure out what it is." She said, no. She told me that she knew what they were referring to but it had nothing to do with numbers on the clock. They still were trying to reinforce for her that she was going to live a long time. She had been obsessing over the number fifty. Neither of her parents and none of her siblings had survived past that age. They were trying to let her know that she would.

Is there any way we can change our date with destiny?

Some people have a very strong sense that they know how long they'll live, whether that comes from specific premonitions or just a gut feeling. But still we have free will, and will always have opportunities to complete our soul's journey for this lifetime. There are times we can, in essence, renegotiate an exit point, even if we are very ill and death seems imminent. I've heard numerous stories about someone who was old or very sick who would be contacted by the Other Side, maybe seeing or hearing a loved one who had crossed, telling them that their time was near. If that person feels strongly there is still something important they must do, they will sometimes be given an "extension." It might be a spontaneous remission, or it might be some other sort of intervention that gives them a new lease on life. *Usually* it's only brief, and it does differ from person to person—I don't know the reason why.

If I get the strong feeling that someone is going to die, and yet that person is not sick or troubled, what should I do?

It is possible that you may be receiving a true psychic message about the person. But unless you have a history of being very psychic, or really, even if you do have this background, my feeling is that I would not say this to a person. It does seem like a double-edged sword—damned if you do (the person might be scared or angry) and damned if you don't (you might end up feeling like you didn't do something when you could have). But in almost all cases, it is not our place to interfere in this, to put our oar in, or try to steer someone else's destiny. The fact is, you could be wrong—your feeling, if it's "true," might just mean that the person is going to make some kind of change or is about to have a new life experience that will, in a way, "end the life" of the way they have been or what they have been doing. What you could do is just ask the person if everything is okay with them. That much you can do. They may seem on the surface like all is great in their life, but there may be something that you don't know about that they are keeping hidden and might be the reason for what you are picking up on. As a friend, you might be able to help that person without saying, "I think you're going to die." When I am doing a reading for someone, if I am getting this kind of message, I will not say, "Oh, they're telling me that they are coming to get you soon." But I might say, "They want you to do X for yourself," something that they know will make that person happy in the time they have left, or, "They are telling you that you should organize your things," which isn't saying "you're outta here" but does give the person the understanding that their time now is more precious than ever. If someone asked me directly: "Are they saying that I'm going to die now?" I would give them a direct and true answer, but that is very different from my taking it upon myself to say it. For someone who is not a psychic, I think you need to tread very lightly in this territory, and above all, ask for spiritual guidance. This is a question for God, not for me.

I had a man visit me for a reading one time who was very emaciated. Also, his stomach was distorted, and it was very pronounced on his extremely skinny frame. It was clear that he was not a well man. I heard the Other Side telling me that he didn't have long at all, but wasn't clear whether he already knew this. Even though I was getting strong messages, I was conflicted as to whether I should tell him something directly. So I made the focus of the reading all about his welcoming committee, all the relatives of his who had crossed who were describing how beautiful it was and how happy they were. I left it up to him to ask me, or not, about his own condition. Finally, he did ask, and I did tell him. Later, after he had died, not three weeks later, his family told me how happy and at peace he was when he died. Knowing that where he was going was beautiful and perfect and that other family members who he loved and who loved him would be there had made all the difference to him.

If someone is not a believer when it comes to the Other Side, how can they overcome their skepticism?

I don't think there is any magic recipe for convincing someone of something they don't want to be convinced of. In my work I meet far more people who do know the truth of the Other Side's existence than I do nonbelievers, but there are also those who just show up to try to prove that they know better, that all the others are deluding themselves or that I'm such a fabulous actress that I have them all fooled with my performance. I'm very happy that I don't see too many of these guys. They should know that I've already been put to the test, so to speak, by my own husband, who, while he never disbelieved in me, did definitely "reserve judgment." I sometimes have said that John was an atheist when I met him. That's not quite true. I know that John always left open the possibility that there was some kind of higher power. He always would say, for example, that we are all made of energy and energy can't be created or destroyed, so he didn't know what happened to us when we died, but he wasn't convinced there was such a thing as Heaven, a place like the Other Side. I think with John, he just wasn't into man-made religions and all the stories and myths that are part of them.

But each person is different in what will speak to them or convince them. For John it was a reading I was doing for a woman at one of my big shows. Her husband came through and what he wanted to tell her was that she could get rid of the fish table. This woman went white as a ghost. Once her friends revived her, it turned out that her husband had had a table made with some kind of fish—I don't recall if she said exactly how the fish was part of the table. But apparently, even though he intended it as a nice thing, she'd never liked this table, yet felt like she had to keep it. After her husband died, she kept it because it reminded her of him, but probably she'd also have felt guilty getting rid of this thing that he'd loved so much. Or, who knows, maybe now she actually cherished it because it reminded her of her husband. So here he comes now from the Other Side to say, "Go ahead, honey, get rid of the fish table—you don't have to keep it anymore." Well, in all the readings I've done there has been many a dramatic story, but for whatever reason, this is the one that reached my husband. As he tells it, it was because it was so ordinary: an ordinary guy, an ordinary woman, an ordinary marriage. In every marriage there are these things that annoy one or the other person, and yet we put up with them because it's part of the package. In a marriage there are things you do for love, to please the other person, even if you have to grit your teeth to do them. In this marriage, it was putting up with the fish table. But now that he had the perspective of the Other Side, this guy wanted to tell his wife, "You don't need to put up with it on my account, you don't have to keep the table." And you know what else? Nothing is that important, nothing material really matters. In the scheme of things, a fish table—or anything else for that matter—is meaningless. This was so simple, so ordinary, but it's the thing that turned John around and really made a believer of him. It was so minor, but so specific. As he told me, even from a skeptic's point of view, it was a thing just strange enough that no one could have come up with it just guessing.

As far as the skeptics go, who knows what will convince one or another? Each person has a different little button that once it's pushed there'll be no going back. Truthfully, even though I really love it when it happens, I'm not out there even looking for those buttons. I'm just doing what I do. Every now and then, I'll meet someone at one of my shows, or I'll get a letter from someone like the one I got recently from a sixty-two-year-old man who told me he wasn't "into" mediums, but his wife put my book on his bed table where he keeps his nightly reading, and he picked it up just meaning to move it off his table, but then just started reading and didn't stop and felt like he really learned something and was convinced. And sometimes someone will tell me about something that had nothing to do with me that they experienced firsthand, which turned on the light for them, and that's why they are now coming to one of my shows. I don't really mind skeptics, so long as they do have an open mind and are willing to see the truth. The only ones that really bug me are the ones who are simply contrarians and even if they do see the truth will call it something else.

I always tell skeptics, "I don't have all the answers. I have *some* of the answers and I just try to do my best with what I've got." I love it, though, when I get something right—even if the real credit goes to the dead guys over there. One day I'd like to see a little Concetta doll—you'd pull the string in the back of her neck and she'd say, "I told you so!"

All kidding aside, it means a great deal to me when I do win over a skeptic. Not because I need them to believe in my abilities, but because I know the peace it gives most people to know for certain that their loved one is always with them, if not in the flesh, in spirit. After a show at Mayfair Farms in West Orange, New Jersey, I was signing copies of my book for those who had purchased it. A gentleman who I'd done a reading for during the show came up to me in turn and I remembered our exchange. He had lost his daughter, and she had come through with a number of validating messages, among which, she'd said that she knew the family cruise was planned and that he'd been thinking he didn't want to go—he didn't feel it would be the same without the whole family; he couldn't imagine being able to enjoy their traditional gathering missing her. His daughter knew this and urged him to make the trip. She told him that she would absolutely be with them. She would always be with him, wherever he was, in spirit. This man said to me, "Concetta, I have to tell you something. I did not want to come to your show today. I didn't believe in this stuff, that the Dead are living and that we can hear from them. But when my daughter told me to go on the cruise, I lost it." He was getting choked up, and so was I. We both had tears in our eyes. He said, "Concetta, you don't know me, but I love you." I said, "You're right. I don't know you. But I love you, too." It's our tears that connect us. That's what makes us all human.

I've heard it said that the light spots that sometimes show up in photographs are actually spirits—is this true?

Yes, that is true. It is not a malfunction in the camera—your camera can be brand-new, it can be regular film or digital, it doesn't matter. Spirits are energy, so they often will show up in your pictures. Little bubbles of lights, also sometimes referred to as "orbs"—these are spirits or souls. Sometimes it seems I can hardly take a shot without one or more getting into the act. One story I heard about: A young woman's father had died, and she was upset because she was getting married and her father would not be there on her wedding day. They didn't hire a professional photographer; she had just some regular pictures taken by family and friends. After the wedding, she dropped the film off at a drugstore or someplace like that and sadly, the facility that had the film burned down. So now she had no photos of her wedding. Then she got a call from a friend who said she still had a roll of film she'd taken, but unfortunately, she'd taken mostly atmosphere shots, of the guests and the cake and so forth. She just had one of the bride in her gown. Lo and behold, when this woman saw the photo, there she is in her wedding gown with one of these glowing orbs right beside her—her father, without a doubt. When I was out in Chicago with producer Glenn Davish and his crew to get footage for a sizzle reel to show to television broadcasters, we had a green screen that I was being shot against so that they could superimpose different things behind me, do some fun effects. It was a very busy but fun day and lots of people on the crew were taking regular photos, besides the taping that was going on. When I saw the pictures of myself against the green screen it was like it was snowing! So many of these orbs—all the spirits—all around me.

When you are doing a reading, what are some of the ways you are able to identify the person who has crossed to the Other Side, and what kind of clues do you get?

As a medium, I am clairsentient, which means that I don't just see images and hear voices, but I will also get physical impressions in my body and I will also often *smell* a spirit I am working with. If a spirit while living was an alcoholic, I'll often get a strong whiff of alcohol. If they were a smoker I smell the smoke. I might also smell a particular aftershave, or sometimes the scent of flowers. I was doing a reading for one of my clients and I suddenly got a whiff of this unusual smell, very strong, and I couldn't place it. I said to my client, "What am I smelling? It smells sort of like medicine." She told me about her child, a little boy, who had a particular disease that caused his body, especially his legs, to be terribly painful. His legs just hurt so bad. The only thing that ever gave him any relief was the muscle rub BenGay. She used to rub his legs with BenGay, which helped him a little, at least. After her child died, she was in a toy store, because she had to pick up a gift for one of her deceased son's former playmates' birthday. As she stood in the aisle of the shop, looking at the different toys and trying to decide what she should get, she suddenly got a whiff of a really familiar odor. Immediately she recognized it: BenGay. She knew even though she couldn't see anyone else in the entire aisle that her son was right there with her. She told me that now, from time to time, she will smell this sweet, medicinal smell and she'll know it's her boy paying a visit. To someone else, it might be an unpleasant smell, but to this woman, it brings comfort.

When I'm doing a reading it's not like being handed a script and going on air to read the news. I'm getting all kinds of clues—names, odors, manner of crossing (which can be given to me verbally in a thought, or I might see an image or feel a sensation in my body), etc. Even when I see an image, I still have a tendency to try to guess what I'm seeing. Often it's better to just simply describe and let my client do the guessing. One time I was telling my clients that their deceased loved one was always with them and in fact had recently been with them at a family event. I said, "He tells me he was just with you at a wedding." They seemed puzzled, had no idea what I was talking about. I said, "He's showing me a girl in a white dress, a wedding." They laughed and said, no—it was their daughter's Communion! I guess that would be a little young to be getting married.

Can a medium listen in to spirits around me anytime she or he wants?

As I go about my day, I can see and hear spirits around everyone. For the most part, without even thinking about it, I am filtering them out. They are really none of my business and I would go completely crazy if I paid attention to all of them. If I am doing a reading, a person is in front of me who has come for the express purpose of receiving messages from their deceased loved ones. Even with them coming to me for this, I'll always still try to ask, aloud, for their confirmation, whether I have their permission to listen to the spirits around them. To me, this is only polite. The messages I'm getting from the Other Side are primarily messages of comfort and love from those whose earthly lives are finished— at least for this time around. While they have concern for us, they have no real concerns of their own, for now. The living, obviously, are still here and still have more business to do here, and it's really not my place to get in the middle of that. It'd be a type of invasion or intrusion. Try to imagine, as an example, if you were invited to a friend's home and you took it upon yourself to invite another friend to come over. The doorbell rings and before your friend can go see who's at her own door, you jump up to go let the second friend in, like you owned the place. It's trespassing. I don't know how else to describe it.

You're always talking about hanging out with dead guys. Don't you ever hang out with dead gals?

That's funny! Well, first of all, I use "guys" loosely just to mean all the spirits. On the Other Side there is no gender, no distinguishing body features because there is no body. We're simply energy over there. When I do a reading the spirit will allow me to know, basically, what they were last time they were here, so I'll say that it's a male figure or female figure, but really the spirit that is communicating with me is neither. So the question of hanging out with guys versus gals is one for the physical plane.

While I'm here, I have to say that even though I'm basically heterosexual and married to a wonderful man, I love to hang out with women. I believe that I've incarnated as female more times than I have as male and I have a strong identification with being female, and I love hanging with my girls—my best friend Mushy, my friend Gingerbread. I really love hanging with women of all kinds—straight or gay. I have a lot of gay friends. In fact, truth be told, I'm only a bucket shy of being gay myself and I don't care who knows it. Some people may like to judge that, but those who do are stupid people. You gotta love them, too. They can't help being stupid. Stupid people don't even know they're stupid. I don't know why it is such a concern for some people that they don't want gay people to be able to marry. Really, what is the big deal? Personally, I don't care if a toaster marries a toaster—so long as it's between consenting adults—or consenting kitchen appliances, as the case may be. Love is love!

Anyway, it's no big deal. As I always say, don't make a mountain out of a mothball.

Not to go on a tangent here, but while we're somewhat on the subject of women, let me share a quote I love from Eleanor Roosevelt. She said that "women are like teabags—you don't know how strong they are until they find themselves in hot water." Isn't that great? I love that.

After you've already done a reading for someone, do spirits ever call you back with things they've forgotten to say?

There are many times when I have to stop and count my blessings and acknowledge how grateful I am to have been given the job that I have. It can sometimes be exhausting, but I really do love my work. Any time I do a reading, whether it's one-on-one in my home office, or at one of my big shows with hundreds of people, I feel good that I'm able to help someone find some peace and hopefully even happiness. But there are definitely some moments that stand out. One of these was at a show I did at Mayfair Farms in West Orange, New Jersey, when I did get something of a return call.

I was heading down an aisle, stopping to do readings as I made my way from the front of the room to the back. I'd been down this row earlier in the show, but having completed one pass of the entire room, I was now going back to do a few more readings for people in this area who hadn't had a chance on my first pass. I was moving quickly since there was not much time left—a wedding party would be coming in soon to take over the room. As I was walking I heard a very urgent voice that I was made aware was coming from a spirit who—well, to be honest, it was a little confusing. I knew he either had committed suicide or was *believed* to have committed suicide. He was saying: "Don't let my daughter leave! Tell her I'm okay! Tell her I'm not being punished!" Of course I had no idea to whom he referred—there were people to my left and right, ahead of me and behind me—so what could I do? I stopped in my tracks and basically made a public announcement: "There's someone right here who I think maybe committed suicide, and he has a message for his daughter." I had to say it twice before a woman right next to me spoke up, saying, "It's me." I was surprised, because I recognized her as someone I'd already done a reading for earlier, and her father had come through, but neither he nor she had communicated to me that he had died by his own hand. I had no idea that, for her, her most important question remained unanswered. But her father knew. I said to her, "Your father wants you to know that he is okay. He's been forgiven; he's not being punished for what he did." Her relief and gratitude were obvious. She had been desperate for this answer but had been too embarrassed to ask it. But her father would not let her leave that day without giving her that peace of mind.

Is there a particular reading you've done that would stand out for you as an especially precious moment?

Oh, boy, there are really so many, but to just pick one, let's see . . . There was a couple who came together to have a reading. I said to them, "Who is George? George is saying something about some furniture, and he's smiling." Well, immediately *they* were smiling, too, and they had to tell me the story. Some years earlier, the two of them had been house-hunting without a lot to spend. They went to see a house being shown by an elderly man, George, who had no family and was getting ready to move into an assisted living facility. While he showed them around, they chatted and they got along really well; they had a warm feeling for each other, and George ended up giving them a price they could afford on the house. When they concluded the deal, George said, "Maybe you could use the furniture, too?" He didn't have enough room where he was going to take it, and even though, as the wife confided, it wasn't their taste at all, they didn't have furniture and couldn't really afford to buy enough to furnish the house, so they agreed to keep it.

Well, time passed, and the wife ran into a woman from the neighborhood who had known George when he lived in the house, and she told the wife that George had passed away. Not long after that, the couple finally had enough money to replace some of the furniture, and they decided to get rid of the couch, for starters. But a few nights before the couch was to go out the door, the wife started having dreams of George sitting on the couch, and she began to feel a little bad about getting rid of it. Maybe it held some sentimental value for him. But then, she reasoned, George wasn't even living anymore, and there was no reason why they should continue to live with a couch they didn't really like, so in spite of her dreams, she called a couple guys to come take the couch away. The day they showed up, they picked up the couch and were going out with it when she noticed that somehow one of the cushions had fallen off, and she heard a voice say, "Look in the couch." She said, "Concetta, you won't believe it. I stuck my hand in the couch and pulled out an envelope full of money! Once I found that, I kept looking and found a total of four envelopes, each containing four thousand dollars—sixteen thousand dollars all together!" As you might guess, she then proceeded to tear up the rest of the furniture, but the couch was the only place she found any money. Clearly, George had no use for the money; he'd had no family, and he'd decided that this young couple were the folks he'd most like to see have it. As my client told me, "You have no idea what that money meant to us at that time!" But George did.

Isn't that an amazing story? I love that one.

What do you think about *The Secret*?

I definitely believe in the concept behind *The Secret*, the law of attraction. It's a real thing, without a doubt. But I think a lot of people have a hard time applying it because they get in their own way. Even if they tell themselves they are practicing the principles of *The Secret*, they are secretly undermining themselves because, in fact, they really don't believe it's possible for what they want to come to them or to happen. I actually practice this all the time in my own life *and I know it works*. It's really amazing what you can do when you want something and put your mind and actions to it. But frequently I'll have clients who will be talking about this: how they tried it and nothing happened. It's frustrating for me because to me it's simple. *ALL Mighty God really wants us to have ALL we want.*

Let me tell you the real secret of *The Secret*.

Let's say someone wanted to be an actress. She's good at it, has the sensitivity to understand and portray a different person's character; best of all, she can cry on cue. But somehow the process just beats her up—and quickly. She thinks, it's too hard, it's not going to happen, it's taking too long. Then she begins to lose confidence and says, "I'm no good, nobody wants me, I suck." And soon enough she decides to do something else and just spins it, "It's not for me." The reality was that she *was* good, but underneath it all, she just didn't really *believe* that even if she tried her hardest it would come to her, and because she didn't believe, she sold herself short way too soon and for dumb reasons. The point where it all broke down was in her lack of belief. If we really, *really* want to get, have, and be what we want, that's where we need to adjust our thinking. I finally figured out a way to explain it so that most of my clients now say they get it, so just let me share the thought here.

Try looking at the thing you want as something that is actually yours (or anyone's) for the taking just as soon as you fulfill certain ordinary requirements. Take, for example, getting a driver's license. When you were thirteen or fourteen years old, you didn't have a license and couldn't get one, either. It's not about you, personally, it's simply not legal for someone your age. But you didn't stress about it, like, "I know I'll never get a license," because you knew with certainty that as soon as you turned sixteen, you'd be eligible, and as soon as you passed the test, the license would be yours. It wasn't like, if you were rich or beautiful you could get one, or if you were good friends with Jodie Foster you could get one. You could only get one by being a certain age and passing the test. Period. Still, you could plan. You could save money for your first car; you could think about how great it would be to get around where you wanted to go without asking your parents for a favor. Once you turned fifteen, you could go to the DMV and pick up the booklet to study for your driving test. Once you turned sixteen you could get your learner's permit, then you'd be off to the races. It's a process. Is it easy? Not necessarily—for some, parallel parking is a piece of cake; others might find it necessary to wear a miniskirt to take their test (I'm just kidding!). Some might have to take the test more than once. But the fact is that the license is obtainable simply by being the required age and doing what is required to qualify. If you can manage to think of your heart's desire in this light—no more or less than getting a driver's license—and just do the steps required, more than once, if that's what it takes, you will succeed. No secret about it. You will do, have, or be what you believe you can do, have, or be.

When a significant other has crossed, how can we continue to honor the bond we had with them?

More often than we would like, one partner in a marriage will cross a significant length of time before the other. A lot of people think that they are morally bound to remain alone after that, lest it appear that they didn't really love the person who has passed on. This really is foolishness from the perspective of the Other Side, and so often this is a message that I'm asked to deliver. This side of the veil—the physical side—is the difficult side, the lonely side. We need all the help and love and companionship we can get. Our loved ones who have crossed want us to be happy. This doesn't mean that everyone who loses a spouse will remarry, but many will and that's really what our deceased loved ones want for us. I can't tell you how often I've been doing a reading and the spirit of a spouse will come through and beg me to tell their wife or their husband to try to find happiness again. Many times they even tell me that they've tried to set something up that their living spouse has sabotaged! When we are happy, we make our deceased loved ones happy, so by all means, if you have lost someone you cared for deeply, do try to stay open to finding happiness again. It's really what they want for you.

This does not apply only to couples, partners in marriage. One of my clients, for example, told me that after her mother crossed over, she would frequently see her. In a way this made her happy, but more often she felt sad. She missed her mother and all she could think about was that she wanted to be with her. The last time she saw her mother, she was on a cruise, lying on a lounge chair, and she saw her mother pass right in front of her. She jumped up and tried to follow her mother, but her mother disappeared, and she has not seen her since. She said to me, "Why is it that my mother has stopped visiting me?" I told her it's because she isn't supposed to want to follow her mother; that's not what her mother wants for her. By discontinuing her visits (or rather, by not allowing herself to be seen) her mother was literally cutting the cord between this side and that. Now my client has a new boyfriend—they met on a blind date—and what's weird is that her boyfriend will sometimes see her mother when, while she was still living, her mother never met her boyfriend. My client said, "Why is that—that my boyfriend, who never even knew my mother, will see her and I can't?" My strong sense is that there is a karmic connection between her boyfriend and her mother. It's most likely that her mother even set up the meeting between her and her boyfriend. It wasn't a coincidence. And he can see her mother because in spite of the connection he has with her mother, he isn't wishing himself to be on the Other Side. They want us to be happy *here*.

You say that they want us to be happy, but what if I just can't get past my grief?

I am asked this question very often: *I'm so sad, I'm so depressed. Why won't my loved one come to me?* There is no one way that everyone gets through the pain of a significant loss. We're all different and all relationships are different, even if we are all human and so share most of the same feelings. Some people just seem to have a huge amount of inner strength. I can tell you that even if you have the genuine belief that our souls still live on on the Other Side, you can still feel tremendous sadness when someone you love deeply makes that crossing before you. We're so used to being able to see them, feel their presence, pick up the phone and talk with them. It's just not the same anymore. But some people are able to console themselves or find new meaning in their loss and go forward with strength and even joy. Not everybody is like that. Many people find it difficult to get past their loss, but nevertheless, everyone must.

Do you have any suggestions for mastering this?

The first thing to remember is that if you are thinking, "It's too hard," you need to change your thoughts. When we tell ourselves that something is hard, the words take on power and reinforce this belief, which only holds us back from living in the present. The idea that we are stuck in our grief becomes a habit, like brushing our teeth—something we are used to doing and so do it every day. You can't let grief become a habit. There is no miracle cure; you need to work on it. You can't have that person back. You need to continue to find happiness in this world until you can join your loved one in the next.

Try to focus on the simple things each day. Don't try to do too much at first, but be sure you do something—get out of your bed or off the sofa if you've fallen into the habit of giving in to grief to such an extent that you don't even want to get up. Give yourself permission to laugh—at yourself, with others—this truly will lighten your load. And remember the power of your words. If you tell yourself you can't, why then of course this is true. You won't be able to. You need to tell yourself, you can, you will. Then that will be true: you can, you will.

Most of us have a very incomplete sense of what we are here to do, but I promise you that wallowing in extended and debilitating grief is not it, and until we pull ourselves out of that place we can't put our feet forward on the road to the rest of our exciting life's journey.

You need to recognize that in everything you have free will. If you continue to grieve, that is a choice you are making. We might have a "reason" for the choice we are making—for instance, we might think that if we allow ourselves to find peace or joy we are sending a message to our deceased loved ones that we don't care about them, or to make it even worse, that maybe we never cared about them. We guilt ourselves. Believe me, on the Other Side, they know it all. They know you care about them; they know in your heart you will never stop loving them. But your focus is intended to be on this side so long as we are here, not on the Other Side. It's never intended that we get habitual about our grief, comfortable in our sorrow. We need to *choose* to remember our loved ones with a smile in our heart and on our face. Take it in steps. If you don't believe that you can get over your grief, at least make the choice not to moan and complain, bringing others down around you. Make the choice not to feel guilty if you smile. You'll be surprised where those little steps will take you over time.

Can't the Other Side help me get over my grief?

The answer, to be honest, is that so long as you are so deeply unhappy, they will deliberately create a separation between you here, and them there. They can't come when we are sad because they know how easy it is for us to wish ourselves there when we are still supposed to be here. They don't want to encourage this—it goes against the plans that are still in place for us, the soul agreement we made before coming here. Look at Anna Nicole Smith—she kept saying, "I want to be with Daniel." She missed her son so desperately, she literally willed herself to the Other Side. I say this without judgment because it isn't my place to judge and I'm not walking in her shoes, but leaving like that is like giving up without finishing what you came to do. Her son never intended that. He had his karma; she had her own.

Our loved ones who have crossed do want to be with us (and in reality they *are* with us, always), but they are finished with their own lessons this time. We still have ours; they can't do it all for us. If we want to reestablish a joyful connection with them, we need to make the effort.

If someone commits suicide in order to be with a particular person they are missing, will they in fact see that person, or will they have ended their life in vain?

When someone chooses suicide, it's almost like the question isn't, did they end their life in vain, but, did they *live* their life in vain? I honestly can't think of a time when suicide is the right answer. That said, I received this question from a reader whose teenage friend wanted to be with his deceased mother and so had shot himself. Yes, I do believe that person did get to see his mother. God is so great and good. Even though that action would certainly go against any agreement that individual made for what he was to try to achieve in that lifetime, even though ending his physical life was like throwing the most precious gift back in God's face, God is forgiving. It's that person himself who will have to learn how to forgive himself for destroying the gift he'd been given. It's really not easy. In our pain and loneliness we sometimes do terrible things that we think will bring us relief. We have free will, even in this. But the story doesn't end there. There's healing that has to be done, and karma that has to be balanced.

Can a medium help me if I am grieving over a loved one?

Sometimes people have the mistaken impression that if they are grieving I can fix them. Honestly, that is not my job. This may not be the best example, but I could say it's like a divorce attorney. Some who come to see him need counseling, but his job is only to divide the property, not heal the divorcing parties. I'm not a therapist. My heart wants to help, but it's simply not my talent. Any counseling I do is the kind you'd get from a friend, based upon my own personal life experiences or things I've been told by the Other Side. Other than that, I'm just "reporting," really, just bringing messages from folks who have passed on.

Very often people who come to see me are in need of healing. They will get only momentary relief from hearing a message from their loved one. They immediately want to make another appointment—no matter how far in the future—and will call and call to see if there is another opening. They want to keep going back to the well, but there's only one thing in the well—the truth that their loved one is still with them. For most, knowing this is enough, but some have been so shaken by their loved one's death that they just can't get over it; they are making their pain a career, ruining all their relationships because of their inability to get past their sadness. A reading is not going to fix those folks. They need someone other than me.

I don't want to be confused about what my job is and run the risk of bringing counterfeit information. If people heal after they see me, it's because they have heard the truth. It's the truth that sets them free—I'm just the conduit. That said, there is a recommendation I can make, which I think is very powerful and has worked for me. Try to visualize yourself with the person you have lost sitting next to you, walking with you, always beside you. Visualize that the person is still there, encouraging you to complete your mission here in the flesh. Picture them as an additional guardian angel *helping* you to complete your mission. After all, this really is the absolute truth of the situation.

Is evil a real thing? If so, can you say why it exists?

I do believe, in fact, I know, that evil is real. People always find it surprising that an all-loving God would even allow evil to exist; it just doesn't make sense to them. However, as horrible as evil is—and there really is nothing worse in the world; how could there be? It's the essence of everything hurtful and abhorrent— evil does serve a purpose. Without evil, we would never be challenged, and without challenges, we would never struggle, learn, grow, and evolve. It's the function of evil to confuse your mind and your heart, to make you believe you are weak or limited. This is the opposite of the truth, but this is for us to learn and overcome by our experiences.

I'm always saying, stupid people don't know that they are stupid. The difference between stupid people and evil people is that evil people don't *care* that they are evil. Not caring who they hurt is the very definition of evil.

I have a favorite medal that was given to me by friends in Mexico. It's fourteen-carat gold and has Pope Paul on one side, Saint Juan Diego on the other. It's on a gold chain with a very secure lobster-claw clasp. I've worn it for four or five years, any time I travel, as a symbol of protection. John and I love to travel, and one of my favorite things is to visit historic sites because I will hear stories from spirits who are hanging around these places for whatever their individual reasons may be. It's really fascinating—I make a point of learning the official history, but I also get a bit of "insider" history that others miss. It's not always pretty, for sure, but I want to know. Last year, John and I made a trip to Germany and we decided to visit Dachau. I'd had mixed feelings about it because I believe that in a past life I died in one of these camps, but as soon as we got out of the car my feelings got a lot less mixed. I was trembling and I just couldn't stop. John said, "You know, we don't have to go in." But we were already there and I felt like I had to, so John walked alongside me—I was so panicked. Just when we got right to the door of the place, I felt my necklace slip off my neck and drop to the floor and I heard a voice say to me, "Pick it up and hold it in your hand, Concetta. You are entering a place of evil." I must tell you, the energy in that place was just about unbearable. You can literally feel the evil trapped within the walls. I want to be clear that the spirits there are not those of the victims. They have moved on and are in a better place, but the murderers are still trapped there.

It is up to each of us to expel evil from our lives by our commitment to its opposite: love.

What happens to all the negativity or evil when someone dies who is cruel, mean, or harmful to others?

Bad energy is "defused," or neutralized and dissipated when such people, in spirit form, enter God's Light. (I'm only talking about a person who has been mean—not someone who has committed murder. Murderers don't even get to enter.) But there is still a karmic debt to pay to those they've hurt. Sometimes they can start paying it back by trying to help those they've hurt if those people are still living on this side of the veil. Otherwise, like with any karma, this is a burden they'll carry into their next lifetime.

If someone hurt us early in life, as in the case of child abuse, can their negativity still influence us after they are dead?

This is entirely up to the individual. With anything that happens to us, we either give it the power or we don't. Once the abuser goes to the Other Side, their negativity is defused. The person left here is challenged as to how they will deal with the aftereffects. You can either use your early sad or negative experience to be empowered or disempowered. You can make the choice to do something better, help others. Nobody is saying that letting go of or transforming pain is easy. For some it can take many years of processing or therapy. Others will be able to more readily distance themselves from events that, as a child, they had no control over. The thing to be remembered is that if someone was in that position for karmic reasons (for example, my own mother experienced terrible abuse in the orphanage where she grew up), it is done. It does not belong to them anymore. What belongs to them is the rest of their life and how they use it.

If someone stole a lot of money from us, like in business, what happens to the unpaid debt? Does it get paid back in a next lifetime?

If the person (or people) who have been affected by this negative action are still here, they need to do their best to get rid of any anger, let go, and simply continue without dwelling on their loss. The person on the Other Side who has committed the crime, once they understand how hurtful they have been, both to whoever they stole from and also to themselves (since now they are loaded down with extra karma), will try to come through with blessings. Will you receive a check in the mail for the exact amount that was taken? Well, that's really not impossible, based upon the way the Other Side works, but it's far more likely that you'll be "reimbursed" in other ways. If you over here are working on your part, getting rid of anger, moving forward, then the blessings will be able to come through. That other person knows what he or she did; they know they owe you. What you don't want to do is set up a wall of negativity that will keep blessings from reaching you. All too often it is the case that once one bad thing happens we dwell on it. When we're focused on the bad, the good can't get through.

Besides killing or abusing someone, or
causing them any kind of physical or
emotional harm, is there one thing that
the Other Side says we shouldn't do if we
want to avoid adding bad karma
to our soul?

I'm really glad you asked this question because I definitely
know the answer. This comes up over and over in my readings:
greed.

Over and over and over again, the thing that tears otherwise
happy families apart, it's so common and contagious, is greed. It's
so amazing to me. Everything will be cool—the family is close,
loving, and sharing—until somebody crosses over. Then all hell
breaks loose. What people will do over money and stuff! Con-
niving and justifying, and like I said, it's contagious. Once one
person starts acting up, then others think, "Well, if I don't grab
what's mine, she'll take it all," and they start acting just as badly.
Even when there is a will, some will find a way to twist things to
their advantage. At least that's what they think; they're acting like
here and now is all there is. But they don't understand the karma
they are adding on.

A dear friend of mine had a grandmother who died and left
her two daughters (my friend's mother and her aunt) money to
buy a beach house. The aunt's husband needed money for some-

thing, and she persuaded my friend's mother to loan her share of the money to help her husband out. Once he got out of his predicament, instead of just giving the money back to my friend's mother, they paid for the beach house—but now they say my friend's mother only gets one third of a share, and her sister and husband *each* get a share! This is not at all what her grandmother intended; the sister's husband wasn't even mentioned—she left the money to her two girls. This is just stupid and greedy and mean—some nice payback for the help my friend's mother gave them. But when they are possessed by greed, people can always think of a justification for their actions, whether it concerns money, a piece of jewelry, or a rocking chair that's been in the family for generations. It breaks my heart to hear these stories. Because of something ridiculous, the relationship will never be the same. And the greedy person will come back next time with a big karmic debt. They risk coming back to have little or nothing.

Not every family behaves badly, of course. I'll also hear in my readings how pleased a spirit is that their family did the right thing with their belongings, how good it made them feel to see that nobody got nutso about stuff or money left behind. Because, don't forget, they are still with us and they do see how we behave over their things. What the Other Side wants us to remember is: *Greed never wins.* You create a loss on this side with your ruined relationships, and on the Other Side with a big karmic debt.

The object here is not to make you afraid of your own karma to the point where you give everything away. I'm only talking about not taking from others what is rightfully theirs, not demanding or manipulating to get more than your share. You just need to keep it in balance. We all know what a little generosity does—puts a smile on your face and another person's.

If we've caused someone sorrow or injury and they have already crossed to the Other Side, how can we get forgiveness?

I do think that saying a truly heartfelt prayer for forgiveness is good for the soul. But even in the absence of that, all is forgiven on the Other Side. Once we cross we have complete and pure understanding—of the reasons why those in our lives behaved the way they did, said what they did, even believed what they did. There is nothing they don't understand, and once they understand, there is nothing they don't forgive. Very often the things we feel most guilty about are very small matters in the scheme of everything else. We worry about so much petty stuff over here. But even things that seem monumental, even things that are literally life and death, those things, too, are forgiven completely.

I once had a client, a woman, who came to me beside herself with worry and guilt. She said, "I've been carrying this guilt for eight years. My mother was in such pain before she died. In the final stages of her illness, it took her three long weeks before she crossed. Every time I went to the hospital to visit her, she begged me to get pills for her so she could end her life. I was so torn. On one hand, seeing her suffer so much was killing me, but when it came down to it, I just couldn't do what she was asking. I just couldn't. I feel like because of my weakness she suffered unnecessarily and I'm afraid she's angry that I couldn't bring myself to give her the help she was begging for." This is such a heavy burden that this woman was carrying! This is not a small thing.

But on the Other Side, her mother does understand. Completely. Not for a moment does she think her daughter didn't care enough about her to help her. She knows that her daughter was acting out of love. As far as she is concerned, not only is her daughter forgiven, there is nothing to forgive.

Can you explain what it feels like to travel out of body?

It's just amazing! You feel light and tingly—you're lighter than a bird, faster than a bird. You can travel through walls or closed doors. It's different from anything we experience in physical form. You're not standing up or lying down or even sitting. I couldn't even describe what "position" it's done in because with no body, there is no position. You're just pure energy. You can see all around you in every direction at once.

My mother was raised in an orphanage, a horrific institution. She was beaten savagely, never given proper food or medical treatment. She was hired out to watch kids, clean houses, and so forth. When she and my father got married, he insisted on buying her a car even though she didn't know how to drive. He told her she had to learn. He said, "For the first time in your life you're going to feel free." My mother told me that he was right, and from the first time she started driving, she never stopped. She said, "I could go where I wanted when I wanted. Those bastards didn't own me anymore." Driving is really like being in energy form—even though you are using the wheel, it's not taxing. In a way, cars have taken human beings to the next level, a way to experience while we're still here a little bit of how it'll be to be out of our bodies. I really believe that the reason so many people like driving is because it's the nearest physical approximation to an experience of being in spirit form.

Can you describe a time when you were out of your body?

One time that comes to mind is when I was in the bedroom one night. I don't sleep well without the burglar alarm set because I'm constantly being woken up by dead people, and sometimes I'm just not sure whether it *is* a dead person walking through my room or whether someone has broken in and wants to tie me up and steal all my favorite *bijoux* (that's French for "bling"). In any case, I came "awake" to realize that I was in energy form. When I'm in energy form, all I need to do is to think that I want to be in a particular place and I'm there. A lot of times I'll decide to go see someone I know so then later I can confirm that I really was out of my body by saying, "Last night, were you wearing your long white nightie with the green stripes, and did you have it bunched up around your waist while you clipped your toenails, with a bag of chips and a glass of wine sitting right next to you?" (Just kidding. But I do like to visit friends this way.) This time, I just thought, "I want to go out in the hallway." This was a little unusual because most of the time, I'll go out the window, since in the hallway I'm likely to meet spirits who have gathered to visit with a loved one who might have an appointment with me the following day, or might still be hanging around from earlier. I really don't like to run into those guys when I'm in that state. But this time, I just floated out into the hall. As I did, I was vaguely aware that I was nervous about triggering the alarm by being out there, but of course it didn't go off. I thought that was pretty cool; I was just like the ghosts who could come and go without setting off the alarm.

Is this astral travel only possible at night?

Time of day is not so important. What's important is that you're in a very relaxed state. One day I was home, around noon or early afternoon. I'd been watching a great movie on DVD and was apparently pretty tired because I fell asleep in broad daylight. At some point, I came partially out of my sleep state and became conscious of the tingly feeling and decided to, in essence, go for a ride. I turned so that I was lying flat on my back because, for me, that's the easiest position to leave my body from. Everything that I did was directed by my thoughts. First I thought, "I want to look at my face, see what I look like when I'm doing this," and so I just looked down from where I was and did that. Then I thought, "I want to go out through the hallway" (this is the downstairs hallway—a different hallway from the one where the dead guys usually hang out), then, "I want to go out over the trees," and each time I thought something I was able to do it. Then I thought, "I want to go to John's job site." But for some reason I couldn't manage to make myself go there. I couldn't figure it out since up to that point, I'd been able to direct whatever I wanted to do. So, in any case, I just floated a while over the trees and then I thought of my brother and I said, "Harold, are you here?" And I heard him answer, "Yes, I am." Then I saw his face, a long ways distant from where I was. It was slowly coming toward me, but then all of a sudden he speeded up—it seemed like at the speed of light!—and his face was instantly just an inch from my face! I was so startled that it snapped me back into my physical body, instantaneously. I felt bad to have reacted that way—see, like anybody, even though I'm used to getting out of my body and having these kinds of experiences, I still have human reactions. Afterward I realized that he was trying to teach me that in spirit form, our actions are as fast as we think them.

What is the furthest you've ever traveled out of your body?

I've had so many experiences where I've left my body and have traveled in energy form and it's not always controlled by any means, I don't always know where I'm going. One of my favorites was just before John and I were making a trip to Germany. We'd never been before and were really looking forward to it. I was in bed and I was dreaming that I was soaring over a very large body of water. But then I suddenly realized that I wasn't dreaming, I was out of my body, in energy form—it's a completely different experience than dreaming, but since I'd been sleeping it took me a moment to understand what was happening. I was traveling at very high speed parallel to, and only inches above, the water. I said, "Oh, no! Water!" Someone (I don't know who) was with me and they said, "Concetta, don't worry. It's not the ocean." I have a fear of the ocean. I have no idea why—maybe a past-life thing. My companion pointed and I looked up and saw a road running alongside the water, so I then knew it was a river. Then I looked to the right and saw an old eighteenth-century village, with a very different type of house than anything I'd seen before, and also a number of ruins. As I soared along, taking all this in, I was thinking to myself, "John and I would love to visit that!" and my companion said to me, "We'll bring you back." I didn't know what they meant.

Three weeks later, John and I flew in to Frankfurt, a very large city, to begin our German vacation. We planned to see as much as we could of the country, but didn't have a set itinerary. We got a car and John took over, picking out a route for us, and off we went. Within a week's time, we found ourselves driving on a road along the Rhine River—this river is vast; it is so wide, 300 ships go down it every day. Suddenly I recognized the scenery—it was exactly the same as what I'd seen a few weeks earlier when I was traveling out of my body, but I hadn't known where I was. Now here were beautiful ruined castles, broken walls poking up out of the ground, some others maintained in better condition, sprinkled among villages that looked exactly like what I'd seen. Whoever it was who said, "We'll bring you back," had kept their word.

Can anyone travel out of body?

Yes, I do think anyone can do it. Maybe not "at will," but under certain circumstances. Most people have had the experience of being partially awake and trying to move, and it's like you can't; you're paralyzed. Or you will try to scream, but it's suppressed; no sound comes out or maybe just a bare squeak. This is because the soul has been out of the body and hasn't yet completely rejoined it, so the directions you are mentally giving yourself to move aren't reaching your physical limbs, even though your subconscious is trying to get it going. Many people will get panicky and try to force the body to respond, and eventually it does. However, if you want to travel out of body, it's precisely at this kind of time that you just need to relax, and rather than trying to force the *body* to move, tell yourself consciously that you want to get *out* of your body. You'll feel and see yourself rising out of the body. You never need to worry about getting back in—we remain connected to our bodies with sort of an energy umbilical cord, just like an astronaut stays connected to his or her vehicle while walking in space. The main thing is not to panic because the emotion of fear is what reels us back in before we're ready to stop sightseeing. Believe me, it's happened to me many times! For some reason, I think my brother Harold likes to mess with me when I'm out of my body. He's got a weird sense of humor. One time I was traveling out of my body and I saw my dad and Harold. Harold looked young, with dark hair, as if it were years ago. He said to me, "We'll be seeing you soon." It totally freaked me out! What did he mean by that? Then my father was smiling. He said, "Not really that soon."

Why do you think some people fear ghosts, while others are fascinated?

Actually, that's an interesting question because I'm always saying that people fear what they don't know, but when I think about it, that's not the whole story, since some people are really intrigued by what they don't know. I guess it boils down to different strokes for different folks. Some people just aren't comfortable knowing that they are sharing space with ghosts. I was reminiscing with Brian, an old client of mine, who came to one of my book signings. He's had several readings from me; he was among the first to come to my home for a reading, a long while ago when I was just getting started. Our house then was nothing but a tiny little box that John was in the process of enlarging. When John built the foyer, the first thing he did was frame it in before he knocked out the wall, so basically there was this "box" surrounding an existing window where the front door would be, and we had to go in and out of the backdoor until that part was done. Brian arrived with his girlfriend. I was doing my readings in the dining room at that time, and I'd shown Brian's girlfriend to the living room to wait for him so he could have the privacy he wanted for his reading. Unfortunately, she turned out to be a little bit of a "Nervous Nellie." We'd just gotten started when she came into the dining room very upset. She said she saw someone waving in the front window. Well, nobody could possibly have been outside that window, because the entire thing was framed in with no door, so I knew the person waving was a dead guy. I tried to tell her it was no big deal, but she was upset.

She said, "Brian, I don't want to stay! I want to go home right now!" Just then we heard a big noise in the living room, like someone had tipped over a big wall of books. Of course when we checked, there was nothing out of place. The noise was to get Brian's attention. His uncle who had died of AIDS and who really loved this boy just wanted him to know he was there. Brian was delighted. His girlfriend—not so much.

Another one of my clients told me that when her mother died, she had not had very much that was worth keeping, and in any case, there really wasn't much that my client needed. But her mother had loved to cook so she thought she'd keep her mother's pots and pans to remember her by. One day, she had to run out to the store for something. It was just a quick trip and she had been back a short time when her sixteen-year-old daughter came downstairs. "Why were you banging on the pots and pans?" she asked. "I was going to come down and ask you before, but then it stopped." My client said, "Honey, what pots and pans? I was out just now." Her daughter was so freaked out, but my client realized it must have been her mother just trying to get a little attention. She went into the kitchen and said, very calmly, "Mother, please don't do that again, you're frightening your granddaughter." I thought this was terrific—people are really starting to get it. We can just talk to the spirits of our loved ones. It's normal. Still, I realize it's upsetting for those who have a ways to go in accepting this.

Have you ever been really frightened by a ghost?

Not "frightened" in the sense of really terrified. But with dead guys it's not just the "fear factor," there's also the "startle factor." Not everybody sees ghosts everyday, and I'll jump a mile when I'm surprised by something, trust me. My nerves are just as bad as anyone else's. Like the time I was out of my body taking a little astral spin and I saw my brother's face getting closer and closer to me. It really startled me because I wasn't expecting to see him, and I just zipped right back into my body. I regretted it, because I would have loved to know what he wanted to tell me, but it was a mental reflex. And then with ghosts there's also the "weirdly annoying factor." I lived at home until I got married, when I was thirty. I have never lived alone, and I know I never could. It would be horrible for me. I'm honestly not afraid of spirits. But that said, there are a lot of weird things that go on around me all the time—lights going on and off, water going on, anytime I'd be home alone. If I didn't have another person living with me so I could get my bearings, someone to ground me, I think I'd go nuts.

Just to give you some idea, one thing I remember was one night when I was living at home and I was going to take a shower before bed. I took my pajamas to the bathroom and sat them on the chair, took my shower, toweled off, and started to get dressed in my pj's. Only problem was, the top was missing. I knew for sure that I had both top and bottom when I went into the bathroom, so I figured someone was having fun with me, but still it was annoying. I had no idea where I'd find the top. I covered up with a towel and went back to my bedroom. I looked around for a while but didn't see anything. I was headed back toward the bathroom and I saw my pajama top hanging from the doorknob on the outside of the bathroom. I had just opened and closed that door to go to my bedroom; I know the top hadn't been there then. If I were going to hang my top on the doorknob—for whatever reason—I would have hung it on the inside, not the outside of the door. I *know* I didn't do this. I didn't really get the joke, but I know *somebody* thought it was funny.

One day I had been working in my office and I got up and was going to go downstairs. I was in the upstairs hall that leads to the stairway. The TV was on in the TV room so there was some noise in the house, but then, right behind my head I heard a tiny little ringing—clear as a bell, no pun intended! I looked toward the stairs. On the wall that runs down the stairs we have a few masks—they are Italian, but were given to me by a friend in Mexico. One of the masks is a harlequin—like a joker—and it caught my eye as I was hearing this little bell sound. I turned around, but there was nothing there. I went back to my office and saw that this little doll that I keep hanging in the window—it wears a little jester hat with a tiny bell on the point of the hat—was sitting on the floor. The bell is really small, so it doesn't ring very loud. Even if the bell had rung when the doll fell, it would not have made such a persistent ringing sound, and I never could have heard it all the way from my office to the stairway—especially with the TV on. I knew it was a dead guy, thinking he was being funny, to ring this bell behind my head.

It probably goes without saying that there are a lot of spirits hanging around my office, since that is where the living come to connect with them. So there are a lot of things that happen there or right around there. One time I was straightening out the magazines I have on a decorative pressed-tin table in my waiting room. Behind me I heard a really loud BOOM! I just about jumped out of my skin—I thought a picture in some heavy frame must have fallen off the wall. I turned around and . . . nothing. Not a thing. It's amazing what they are able to do energetically to create a big noise like that. I have no idea how they do it.

Another time, I heard this woman laughing really loudly in my hallway. Oh. My. God. I was so completely freaked out. I knew it was a spirit, but at the same time, the sound of it was so crazy and eerie! No, living alone would never work for me. Once, when I was twenty-five, I thought, I really should move out of my parents' house. I was determined. I went out and found a nice apartment, rented it, and set about making it just the way I'd like it. I put in new carpet, and I bought new furniture to make it really nice. I kept that apartment nine months, paying the rent, without ever moving into it. *I couldn't.* I finally let it go, sold the furniture, and just stayed where I was.

Have you ever been startled by a spirit who came through while you were doing a reading?

Not really, because I'm in the frame of mind where I'm expecting someone, and I'm not sure who, so I'm really in a state of anticipation. It's usually when I'm not thinking about it that I get surprised—just makes sense, right? In any case, when I'm doing a reading, it's more like I'm getting a thought, and any visual is more like a dream sequence or like pictographs on a cave wall, like the Anasazi did in New Mexico. If I say, "It's someone who was a flute player," it's because I see an image of someone holding a thing that looks like a flute he's blowing into. I'm busy assembling a puzzle and they are trying to communicate something specific—they're not playing games in that moment.

What's the craziest ghost story you've ever heard or experienced?

Most of my ghost experiences have not been too dramatic, considering that I talk with the Dead on a regular basis. But if you don't have my background, even a "mild" ghost could be a little much, I suppose. I've heard some crazy ghost stories in my time, but one of the weirdest was the story of my friend's house. She's Italian, first generation here. Her parents moved from Italy, bringing all seven of their kids with them, and they were completely broke when they got here. Luckily, they found a super-cheap house they could rent. Even though it wasn't very big for nine people, they signed a lease and moved in. Right away they begin to notice strange stuff, noises and things. But pretty quickly it went from a little strange to really crazy. (They found out why the house was so cheap!) They'd see a woman sitting on the end of the bed; their pajamas would go missing and they'd find them neatly folded on the sofa, nowhere near where they'd been left. One time my friend's father searched the house high and low until he found his tool box sitting smack in the middle of the basement floor—impossible, since he'd never taken it down there; he always left it next to the front door so he could grab it and go when he went to work. As anyone could imagine, this was pretty spooky for the family, but they didn't have the money to move. One day they heard banging in the kitchen and they ran to see what was happening, only to find that all the cupboard doors were opening and closing on their own, and *still* they didn't feel they could leave the house, even though it really was getting pretty terrifying. Finally, the last straw: the family was sitting together in the living room, all the kids hunkered down on the couch, and all of a sudden, the couch literally rises up off the floor! It levitates to about a foot off the floor—with all the children still sitting on it—and then comes slamming down with a BOOM! The whole family was scared out of its wits, and finally realized that no matter how difficult it would be to find a new place, no matter the cost, they had to get out of there. They later found out that a woman had committed suicide in that house. All I can say is, thank God they were renting!

Is an exorcism the only way to get rid of an unwanted spirit?

No, not at all. Many times a spirit wants to be on their way regardless of whether their presence is bothering us or not. It's not usually their intention to be a nuisance—most spirits want to be near their loved ones, not a stranger. Sometimes they just get stuck and need a little help to get going. A young woman I met in New York, a friend of a client, has a funky light switch in her kitchen. You sometimes have to force it a bit to get the switch to go up, but once it's up it stays up. It's only a minor hassle so she never did anything about getting it fixed. One evening, she was on the phone with a friend and all of a sudden, the light goes off. This never happened before so the first thought in her head is that the wiring must be in worse shape than she thought and she better get it looked at. She goes over, thinking she'll need to jiggle the switch or something and sees that the switch is down. Very strange. It often takes some effort to get it to go up, but it never has just flicked itself down before. She flicks it up and continues talking with her friend, and don't you know the light goes off again! This time when she sees that the light somehow has flicked itself down again she says to her friend, "I better get off the phone!" She's a little freaked out and decides to call another friend, a clairvoyant who lives in California. She tells him what's been happening and he says, "Since I'm not there, would you like me to ask a spirit who sometimes helps me to look into what is causing this?" His guide (who presents herself as a female spirit, even though in spirit form we really are neither gender) goes through the young woman's apartment and reports that there was a man who had died in the apartment, and she is being shown water, so it's likely he died in the bathtub. She convinces this unhappy spirit to leave the young woman's space—but not before he flicks the light switch down one more time! It's great if you have a psychic buddy or your own spirit sidekick who can take care of these kinds of things for you, but the truth is that it's not even necessary. You only need to remember that any time you want a bad spirit to leave you alone, you only need to mention God's name. Just say, "In the name of God, be gone." He's the big guns.

When you do a large show, is there a particular kind of room that is most conducive to the spirits?

The very best setup for me would be a room with lots of air and lots of light. This is not just for large shows—I have my home office set up this way. I have double-hung windows on both sides, and I use a glass table. My sister-in-law Choi explained to me that the arrangement of the furniture I have is compatible with good feng shui—the energy flows easily around my things, there's no clutter, the energy is constantly moving and cleansing—nothing gets stuck. Basically, the lighter the better is my rule—and I like it if there is an open door that I can look out of. Often newer buildings are better. Older buildings were built to keep in the heat; their windows tend to be small, and if they are stone, the energy will get stopped. Interior spaces in these buildings tend to be smaller, so that it's not so easy to get around in physical form, much less energy form.

When I first began to work publicly, sometimes people would ask me to their homes—they'd set me up in a basement—you know, cement floors, windows above, thick walls. They'd light a candle and think I'd be happy with the setup. I didn't have the heart to tell them it wasn't really a user-friendly environment. Another thing that would happen frequently would be that someone would basically throw a little party in their living room and have me in some upstairs bedroom with a little window and a little candle, while everyone else was downstairs with nice snacks, socializing. Not fun for someone like me, who loves being at the center of the party!

But no matter the room, the spirits will still find a way to get in and get their messages to their loved ones; it's just that some present more challenges than others. When I did a show for the Learning Annex in New York City, they put me in a gymnasium. There were windows, but they were small and way up above my head, and there were mats hung on the walls—probably to keep people from getting hurt if they smacked into a wall, but for my purposes it had a deadening effect (no pun intended), but the Dead still got through. I did a large show at Mayfair Farms, in West Orange, New Jersey, which was an absolutely gorgeous venue, but I was in a ballroom with mirrored walls that made the energy bounce all over the place and wrought havoc with our microphones. My sound guy, Chris, has been with me a long time, so he's pretty much seen it all. He said, "We're gonna have to get Dead-proof mics!"

If someone wanted to host a medium in their home, what would be the ideal setup?

Basically the environment should be bright and as open as possible—no basements, no attics, nothing closed in, dark, or boxy. Lots of windows are better; houses that have a lot of steel or stone, not so good. If the gathering is a party, don't greet the medium at the door with a glass of wine. Alcohol impairs spiritually as well as physically, so you don't want her or him to drink before or during the readings—maybe after!

What are some of the coolest things dead guys have done for you?

Oh, that's a good question! They help me out all the time! One of the best things is that they just make me look good by feeding me lines when I'm doing a reading or a show. Some of them also flirt with me and say nice things about me—and no, it's not just all in my head! Though to be honest, after the age of fifty, I'll take a compliment anywhere I can get it—even from a dead guy! Actually, we have a Mutual Admiration Society. They tell me, "Concetta, you are just the bee's knees!" And I say, "Right back atcha, baby!"

I really like it when I hear about them helping others—and this takes so many different forms I couldn't begin to cover them all. Often it can be something as simple as just making a connection and letting someone know that they are there, in a way that can't be missed, so they'll have that comfort. I have dear friends I've talked about before, the Barones, Rachele and Joseph, and their kids, Antonio and Susie. I love them like family. They own and operate the restaurant The Top of the Park. The food is fabulous and they are wonderful. Rachele and Joseph have a farm that John and I like to visit. This past spring we were there and there were brand-new little baby goats, just born, and I got to hold and pet them—Heaven! Rachele is from Italy and has the accent—I love to imitate her: "Concetta, just taste this—I knooow you like this." But she gets in just as many jabs, she'll say, "I know what *you* like—ravioli, Fendi bags, and dead people!" Rachele moved to the United States when she got married, leaving behind her parents and her favorite aunt and uncle, Zia Lucia and Zio Guilio. Some time later, Zia Lucia died, and a little while after that, Rachele was getting ready to make a trip back to Italy. Just before she went, she had a dream in which Zia Lucia told her to buy a necktie, which she understood was to be a gift for her Zio Giulio. Her aunt was impressing upon her that the tie should be of a particular shade of blue, patterned with paisley. The dream was so powerful and real to her that she thought, why not? She went shopping and lo and behold, she found a tie exactly like her aunt had shown her in her dream and she bought it. She took it with her to Italy and gave it to her uncle Guilio. When he saw the necktie he started to cry! He told Rachele that the last thing he'd bought for Lucia was a dress in that very same fabric and print. This was no coincidence. There is not a doubt in my mind that Lucia wanted to let her beloved Guilio know that she was still with him.

Another super cool thing the dead guys did for me seemed more like a favor they were doing for John, but any time they help one of mine I get the same charge, like it's a personal favor. A couple months ago, John and I went out for a meal and to do some shopping. When we got home John realized he didn't have his reading glasses. This is no small deal. These reading glasses are truly one of John's prized possessions—they are Dolce & Gabbana that he bought in Paris on one of our trips. He *loooves* them and has often said that he knows he'll never find anything like them again. We'd only gone to two places—a little restaurant and to Marshall's—so he just figured he'd backtrack and maybe get lucky. He went back to the restaurant and told the owner where we'd been sitting, but nobody had found and turned in his glasses. Next he races back to Marshall's and looks all over where he'd been looking at shirts. He's like a lunatic—looking under the tables, in the bins—but he doesn't find the glasses. He goes back home dejected, he's slouched down in his chair in this terrible funk. But you have to know John. It's only partly because of losing the glasses. The bigger part is that he's really down-hearted about mankind, because he's sure that somebody found the glasses and thought, "Wow, cool glasses," and just kept them, and John would never do such a thing. He can't understand how anyone would take—or even find and just keep—something that isn't theirs. I'm trying to cheer him out of his mood, I ask, "Are you okay?" He says, "I'm fine." But he really is not fine and I can't stand seeing him this way. So now *I* go back to where we've been before. I know he's already looked, but I think, maybe I can get some extra help. I ask the Other Side, "Come on, guys, can you help me out with this? John really loves those glasses. Whaddaya say?" I go and ask again at the restaurant if maybe they've turned up since John was there. No dice. Then I go to Marshall's. I look all around the shirts and I even go to where they have sunglasses on display, thinking that maybe someone picked them up and put them back on the rack with the glasses. Nada. To be honest, I'm not looking forward to going home and seeing John in his funk, but I can't think where else to look. Again I call over to the Other Side and say, "Please, can't you come up with something? Please help me find the glasses!" Anyway, I get home, park the car, I'm going inside, and I hear a spirit whisper to me, "Concetta, turn your head." I look over to the left and there on a rock next to the door are John's glasses. How they got there I don't even want to try to figure out! I was just delighted. I love when something like that happens. I love when I get to say to John, who still remains a bit skeptical even after all this time with me, "John, what are you going to do if I tell you the Other Side brought you something that you really want?" I never get tired of that. And John was never so happy!

Lots of times dead guys (and gals) have come to my rescue. I'm not talking about being in actual danger—I've already mentioned that thing we call ESP that is actually our protectors cluing us in that maybe we shouldn't trust a particular person, that they mean us harm—just out of a bad spot. One time that comes to mind is when John and I were traveling in Colorado in 1995. We wanted to stay at a beautiful old hotel there, the Stratford, but foolishly we hadn't called ahead for reservations. When we got there, they were completely booked up. It was a holiday weekend and we didn't have any idea how far we'd have to travel to find another place. The manager was very nice and very apologetic, but we realized it was our fault for not planning ahead. The Stratford has a gorgeous old saloon, and we decided to sit in there to regroup. We told the manager that we understood it was unlikely, but if anything came up, we'd be there in the bar. A historic building, the saloon was rich in souls—exactly the kind of place I like to visit because I often will hear very interesting stories being whispered. As we sat talking, I heard a few of the spirits saying, "Don't worry. Something is coming for you." I told John, and he said, "Really?" Smiling, I said, "Yep. Just got the call." In a few minutes the manager came to find us, pleased to let us know that he'd just gotten a cancellation on a suite—which he let us have for the price of a regular room since we'd been so nice and patient.

It seems like the Dead enjoy helping out—why is that?

Okay, I know not everyone is the same—on the Other Side we are just as unique and individual as we are here so there are bound to be a wide variety of answers to this question. But I'm going to take a leap here and say: *because they can.*

It's like Henry David Thoreau said: "To affect the quality of the day, that is the highest of arts." Don't we all like to do nice things for those we care about? Once we're over there, there are a whole lot more people that we care about. Definitely we are each tied to particular souls in a special way, but we also understand that we are all one, and we see the ripple effect of every good deed. From the Other Side, the Dead see everything clearly. They see how all the pieces here fit together, who did what for whom and why. And I really think they do appreciate any nice thing anyone did for them while they were here.

At one of my big shows in New Jersey I was moving down the aisle to speak with someone near the back of the room, but I came smack up against this wall of energy, or rather sound. This is a little hard to describe, but it's actually more an "audio" phenomenon than a physical one. It's a matter of a soul getting so loud that I can't hear anything else. When I can't hear properly I get confused. They stop my stream of thought, like when you are talking to someone on your cell phone on the street and you walk by a jackhammer doing roadwork, or an ambulance or fire truck goes by. So there was a very powerful spirit who did not want to let me pass until I found his loved one and allowed him to pass on a message. It didn't take me long to identify his wife right next to where he'd stopped me in my tracks. He was a very odd energy, very forceful, maybe trying to be funny, but not really succeeding, or succeeding in a weird way. He was a character. He wanted me to tell his wife he was saying thank you to her because all his life he had been misunderstood. She was the only one who really "got" him. In a very real way, she protected him. A lot of times he'd find himself in the middle of some situation because of something he'd said or done and she'd be the one explaining him out of it. She'd say, "He didn't mean it like that, it's just his way, he has a good heart," and so forth. He knew she always did that for him and he appreciated it. He wanted to be sure she knew how much he appreciated it. Poet Maya Angelou once said, "I've learned that people will forget what you said, people will forget what you did, but people will never forget how you made them feel." That seems right to me. We all want to feel understood and loved. And we remember those who have made us feel that—even after we've crossed to the Other Side.

What would you suggest to make the world a better place?

Here's one of the advantages the dead guys have—from their bird's-eye view of all that's going on, they can see the real truth of the saying, "What goes around, comes around." They understand karma, and they understand the beauty of a good turn or just simply being a nice person, respectful of others' feelings and rights, appreciating what we have and not trashing stuff thoughtlessly. But we don't have to cross over to grasp this! We just need to open our eyes, wake up! I have to say, it may not be my business to be so, but I am really the Bad Behavior Police. Any chance I get, I'm going to use my voice to tell people, *You gotta try harder! You gotta get it together, baby!* I can't stand when people are inconsiderate of others or of our planet. Every day you see people who have no patience with overworked service personnel in restaurants or stores, drivers who don't use their blinkers, the person at the end of the line who sees a new cashier opening up and rushes to claim the quick check-out that somebody else has waited a long time for, people who can't seem to manage the words "thank you," folks who throw their candy wrappers and empty cardboard coffee cups down like they think maid service is gonna be by right behind them, people who park so close to someone else's driveway that they can't get their car in their own garage, or park in front of their door so they can't get out. To them I say, "Look around! Pay attention, make the world a better place." I have a big mouth. I see some kids with dirty hands running behind their mother in a Target store, pulling clothes off the racks, and I tell them that's not a nice thing to do. Don't you know, their mother turns around and instead of asking her children to pick up and put back what they've pulled down, she tells me, "Don't tell my children what to do!" To which I reply, "These children have very bad behavior, and now I know where they get it." Okay, I don't make a friend every time I open my mouth. But maybe those kids will think about this, even if it's lost on their mother. Maybe those kids will see other examples, besides what they experience at home, and realize it's up to them, it's up to each of us, to make the world a better place.

I'll get off my soap box—I realize it's not my place to be the judge. But like I'm always saying, I'm not perfect. We can all stand a little improvement. I personally try to be open to constructive criticism. It all depends on how it's given—I prefer calmly and lovingly, without yelling, swearing, or physical violence. If it's really intended to help me, I can take it. I've got my big-girl underpants on.

Why is it that we are not supposed to judge?

It's crazy—we all are making judgments every day, but we're really only judging ourselves, and the only real judge is God. I know how *I'd* like things to be, you know how *you'd* like things to be. We both know your opinion and mine aren't going to jive 100 percent of the time. Bottom line, things are gonna be the way each of us makes them. And we each have to make our own mistakes. If I learn from seeing someone else's mistake so I don't have to do that one, I'm still going to make a different one—there are plenty to go around, plenty of lessons for each of us. Coming back from doing a TV taping I was talking with the driver—actually, I was venting about some dumb thing that someone had done—a woman acted all nice as pie on air, but made mean remarks when the camera was not on her—and he said something that I thought was really wise. He said, "Concetta, never judge your own intelligence against other people. There will always be people who are smarter than you and there will always be people who just don't get it—no matter what the subject. Using yourself as a measure to judge others' intelligence will only lead to disappointment." Good lesson.

I've mentioned a number of times in this book that I know I'm not supposed to judge, or that I try not to judge. It's one of those things that I know intellectually, but still struggle with. I think a lot of us do.

A friend of mine took up running at a later age. She likes to mull over all kinds of stuff when she runs and one thing she told me that I liked was something that came to her while doing laps around the reservoir in Central Park. When she first started running she used to get annoyed with herself if someone passed her and a little gleeful when she passed someone else. She finally realized that neither passing nor being passed was a knowable measure of anything. Why should she feel happy if she passed someone who looked twenty years younger than she? They may be just getting back at their running after a serious injury. Why should she feel bad if someone passed her on her third lap—it might be only their first. She rarely knew when and where another person came onto the track and could not know how far they had run to get to the track or what heavy baggage they brought with them onto the track. Any judgments made about another runner and how she compared to them in the moment of passing or being passed were meaningless. Instead, she realized, the fact that they were on the track at all meant that they were showing up, just as she was, to make an effort.

It's the same in life. We're out here playing the game as best we can. If we happen to see someone dropping the ball, it doesn't mean they're a consistently bad player. Maybe they just twisted their ankle and deserve our sympathy, not our judgment. The only one who knows our whole journey is God. The only one who knows what is in our heart of hearts is God. The only one who gets to judge us is God.

What if we don't need anything—will our loved ones still be around us?

Oh, yeah! The Dead get a kick out of us. We're like television to them. They love watching their kids, the grandkids. They love seeing us try new things, working out our problems, falling in love, playing. When I'm doing a reading, they tell me all kinds of things that they love. Like, a grandfather told me he likes to stand behind his little granddaughter when she's practicing the piano. He likes to try to get her to play in the old-time style that he loved when he was here. Or they'll observe how much they appreciate that something of theirs has been saved and is being used. A grandmother might notice that her stitchings have been saved, all the little table drapes or towels she stitched. They may have a gravy stain or two, but that doesn't matter. She made 'em, you saved 'em; she loves that. These seem like little things, but they mean a lot to them. They love when we continue to get use from things they've left or to remember traditions that were cherished by them in life. You can't take it with you, but observed traditions or things that a soul loved in life and are held dear by a descendant have transcendent meaning.

Are the Dead proud of their earthly accomplishments, of things they've done or created that they leave behind them?

Yes. Yes. Yes. Yes. It's like any kid who goes to school to learn something specific that will help them to get a better job or have greater opportunities. Once they have that diploma, they think about all the hard work they put in to earn it. It's meaningful to them, a real source of pride. They made the effort; they will have the reward. Our accomplishments here, whatever they consist of—whether it is raising a good kid, or writing a Broadway musical, or doing the research that leads to the cure of a disease, or building a home, or whatever—there is some result that the individual is proud of, but even that is just the outward, visible part of all that went into it. Countless thoughts and countless actions. It's all meaningful; it's all important. And yet, as meaningful as those things are, the true accomplishments are soul accomplishments, the different ways the person has grown spiritually through all of it. And those accomplishments are between the individual and God.

Can the spirits of our deceased loved ones come to us in dreams?

They certainly can and often do. I recently received an e-mail from a woman who said the night before her last birthday she was depressed. It wasn't one of those landmark birthdays, like the big 3-0 or the big 5-0, that we think of as being traumatic; it's just that she noticed age was creeping up on her and she wished she had her mother with her. That night she dreamed that her mother was spending her summer in Portugal as she used always to do. In the dream, the phone rang and she recognized her mother's voice. Excitedly, she said, "Mommy, you remembered me!" and her mother replied that she would never forget her. When she was living, she always called the children on their birthdays.

How can we know if it's really our loved one or just something we "dreamed up"?

The brevity and clarity of the incident I just described suggests strongly to me that it was an actual visit. If your dream is convoluted with a lot of confusing scenes or moves from one setting to another, or if it contains bizarre elements like a pink elephant or a movie star on a Ferris wheel, then more likely than not this is "just" a dream. Psychologists will tell you that you are everyone in the dream or that everyone in the dream represents some aspect of you—this is how we sort out our day's stresses; our subconscious produces these scenes to flush out things that are bothering us. Often, they don't make any sense to us on the surface and need to be interpreted before they are of any value to us. It's pretty easy to tell this kind of scenario from a true visitation. A visit from the Other Side will be striking and obvious, short and sweet. You see a real person who you recognize. They may say something, but these messages are never long or complicated. You may not even be able to hear what they say—maybe you just see them moving their mouth and you can't make out the words. Or you may even just see them waving. No pink elephants. No movie stars. No interpretation necessary.

An example that comes to mind is a client of mine who told me that when she was in college, just before leaving for Christmas vacation, she had a dream that her grandmother came to her to say that she wouldn't be with the family at Christmas, but that my client shouldn't worry, her grandmother would be okay. Just that. A simple, clear message. When she arrived home, her family told her that her grandmother had died the previous week. They hadn't wanted to upset her while she was taking her final exams before the holiday so had not told her that her grandmother had passed away.

Is it normal for a loved one to visit in a dream before they cross to the Other Side?

Near the time of death it's not uncommon for the spirit to separate from the body and visit a loved one, and this may transpire while their loved one is in a dream state. One of my clients told me about how one night her husband was working and she knew he wouldn't be home right away, so she went on to bed without him. She was sleeping when she dreamed she heard a knock at the door. In the dream, she got up and went downstairs to the door and opened it and saw her husband standing there wearing a hospital gown. As she stared at him he said, "Honey, I'm going to go home now," and he disappeared. The dream was so vivid and startling that she woke up and got out of bed. She got dressed even though she didn't really know what she was going to do. She went downstairs and was sitting in the living room when there was another knock at the door, and this time when she answered it, there was a policeman standing there. He told her that her husband had been in an accident and he would bring her to the hospital where her husband had been taken. When she got to the hospital, there was her husband, dressed in a hospital gown, just like she'd seen him when he came to the door. Five minutes later, he died. Just like he'd told her, he went home.

Is one religion more "right" about the Other Side than others?

I would say, no. Inside all of us we all know the truth about God and the Other Side. All religions are structures that can help to bring the truth to the surface and make it conscious. Throughout history, truth has been distorted. Spirituality is the pathway that connects the heart and the soul to the essence of God. Through that relationship, the truth will come out.

How is it that we've gotten so far from Heaven, from the side of God?

While we are in the body, our focus is here in the material world, where our senses rule. We're focused on what we can taste, feel, buy, and sell. Our challenge is to remember the spiritual, even when it is hidden by all the glitter of the world. It's not impossible, but it does take effort. Realize that God and his angels and all his miracles did not leave us and never will. Many have just stopped making them a priority. It's up to us to refocus and reclaim our connection.

Why is it important for us to find our spiritual nature?

It is vital that we realize we are a spirit in a bodily wrapping. When we connect to our spirit, we connect to our true self. If we stay focused only on our human mind and our emotions, we run the risk of being trapped in a shifting and insecure personality. A wise person once said, "When we are born, we are embodied spirits. What we are to do with our lives is to become spiritualized bodies."

Why do you feel it's important to do the work you do?

I hope that this work helps to clear away the illusions and confusion people have about what life really is like and what our human experience is meant for. If we choose to remain in the belief system that being human is only about "Earth," this place where we live in our embodied form, and other things we can touch or see, we'll remain stuck in fear. We'll have so many fears and problems and unanswered questions, and we'll try to solve our problems with means that do not look first to love (God) and that only add more karma to our spirits. Evil, harm, injustice, atrocities—all are "Satan," or whatever you want to call it (in the Jewish tradition "Satan" means "the adversary," whatever works against good). All these things exist in this world. The way to dismantle these negative systems is for more and more people to stay strong and live in the principles of truth and love. By opening the door from this side to the Other Side, we have access to God's world and His reasons for this world. I want people to know that nothing is final about death. I want people to be comforted and reassured and live a fuller life by knowing that even at the "end" of that life, nothing ends.

When we dream of the Dead, are they really trying to talk to us?

Indeed they are! Because we are in the subconscious state, they can have a nice conversation with us without our being freaked out. When we are awake we tend to hold very tightly to our construct of what is normal and possible—which is an incredibly limited view compared to what the true reality is: to what truly not only is *possible*, but just *is*. When we are in this nice relaxed state, we allow the true reality of our oneness with spirit to just be, and spirits will use this opportunity to connect with us.

What is the biggest secret you've learned from the Dead?

That's an easy one: what you ask for you shall receive. I love this story—it's been told in many different ways and to a lot of my readers I know it'll be very familiar, but here goes: Mr. Manicotti had lived a good life and was reasonably satisfied at the end of it. He hadn't been rich, but he'd always had "enough"; he'd had good friends, a loving wife and kids. All in all, not bad. When he died, not surprisingly, he ended up in Heaven where he met Saint Peter at the gates, just as he'd expected. Even though it's what he expected, he's thrilled. Heaven is all he thought it would be. So now Saint Peter is giving him the tour and here and there he's seeing old friends and family he hasn't seen in years, and he is being greeted by his old well-loved and remembered pets. Heaven is a terrific place and there's a lot to explore. Up ahead, Mr. Manicotti sees a beautiful white building and he tells Saint Peter he'd like to go see it, but Saint Peter says, "No." This is surprising—he hasn't expected to be denied anything in Heaven. He asks Saint Peter why this building is off-limits, but Saint Peter just tries to steer him in another direction. Needless to say, this makes him more than curious. He says, "Please. I'd really like to see what's in that building." So, reluctantly, Saint Peter takes him over to the building and they go inside. There Mr. Manicotti sees rows and rows of shelves, filled to the brim with glittering boxes, each marked with the name of a soul. He runs over to the shelves and searches to find his own name, and sure enough he discovers a hefty box, gorgeously wrapped, that is clearly intended for him. As he's reaching for it, however, Saint Peter says, "Don't open it. If you look inside it'll only make you weep." "Why on earth?!" asks Mr. Manicotti. "Because," says Saint Peter, "in that box are all the blessings and gifts that God had prepared for you, if you had only asked."

The moral of the story is: Think Big, Dream Big, *ASK* Big. God wants us to be as big as He is. That's what it means to be made in God's image. We will never be as big as God, but so long as we don't dream big and ask big we will always be smaller than we can be. Never be afraid to ask for blessings—both in your prayers and in your daily words and actions. There is more than enough of everything to go around. God's blessings are infinite and eternal.

ACKNOWLEDGMENTS

John Bertoldi, aka Johnny Fontaine, Juanito, and so many other names I cannot mention: My beautiful husband, you have been an enormous support and comfort to me for twenty-five years. Our life together has been anything but boring! Because of you I have enjoyed true love. Thank you, Jaunito. I will love you for many lifetimes.

Eleanor Ferrell, my mother: My heart is full of admiration for you and all you survived in your early childhood. Thank you for being a wonderful mother and making unselfish choices. I completely love you.

Cornelia DiNunzio, aka Mushy: I still remember that little girl I met more than forty years ago. We have spent a lifetime going through so much joy and sorrow. I cannot imagine my life without you in it, you have given so much of yourself to me. A sister you are and always will be to me. I love you.

Robert Ferrell: My brother, my sweet handsome brother. I have always found you to be kind and compassionate. You always believed in me and said I could do this. Thank you for seeing that. Harold would be so proud of the life you made for yourself, as I am. I love you so very much.

Choi Eng: My sister-in-law, you are a fantastic contribution to our family. Thank you for everything you have done for our family. God loves you, and so do I.

Elena Oswald, aka my sweet Elen baby: You don't have a mean bone in your body. How lucky I am to have you in my life and family. You have kept me calm and cool with you at the wheel. I treasure our relationship. I love you.

Madeline Krawse: My dear friend, I thank you and Steve for so many kinds words and laughs we've shared on Friday nights over dinner. Getting away to the lake and swimming with ducks, all the generous things you say and do. It was a great day that you came into my life. I love you both very much.

Stephany Evans, aka Tex: My dear friend and agent, I remember the day I met you in 2003, that cold day in New York at the Gersh Agency. It was my lucky day. I still remember your laugh, which I still enjoy today. I love you with all my heart. I will thank you forever for seeing something in me.

Ginger Grancagnolo, aka GG or Gingerbread: I have borrowed so many of your words and thoughts. I admire your strength and heartfelt passion. I never get tired of your stories or your insights into the Other Side. I love and adore you—the little girl in you and the little girl in me are best friends. Forever.

Rachele Barone: My sweet Italian friend, it is a comfort to know you care about me. I thank you for bringing me food when I was not feeling well and for all the extras at dinner. The very sound of your voice makes me feel at home. I love you.

Jessica Bertoldi (Franchina): My adopted daughter, we have come such a long way. I will always have the image in my head of a little girl in a ponytail, so full of life, eleven going on thirty. I am proud of you. I treasure our relationship. Thank you for calling me Mom. I love you.

Johnny Bertoldi Jr.: You have grown into such a beautiful man. I appreciate all of your Mother's Day cards. If I had had a son, I would have wanted him to be you. I love you, sweetie.

Darlene Bertoldi: Having met you twenty-five years ago, we

have seen a lot together. Here you are all grown-up with children of your own. I am proud of you and the wonderful job you do as a mom. I thank you for the many times you have listened and given comfort to me. I love you.

Lorenzo Franchina: My son-in-law, some people come into your life late and feel like they have been there forever. Thank you for writing that beautiful poem about me. The only other person who ever wrote a poem about me was my father—you are in good company. You will never know what that meant to me. I love you.

Jennifer Pooley: My senior editor at HarperCollins, with vision! We have become very close and shared our lives; for this I am grateful. Thank you for believing in me. I wish only the very best life has to offer for you, always. I love you.

Audrey Harris: My senior publicist at HarperCollins, you have always had my best interests at heart from the start. Thank you for all the dates and times you have arranged—a job well done! You have had patience and shown kindness—both meant a lot to me. I love you.

Glenn Davish: You have done so much for me, and I cannot believe how lucky I am. I thank you for all the wonderful times we have shared together. I look forward to the future and the adventures we have to go on. I love you.

Tim Ousey: Thank you for the refrigerator full of my favorite things and the bowl full of candy—you think of everything! Glenn is lucky to have you in his life. I am lucky to have you both. I love you.

Jon Cornick: You will always mean the world to me. I love you.

Sarah Self: With your interest and introductions, you set off an amazing chain of events in my life. Thank you—I'll never forget you! I love you.

Alexander, Julia, Isabella, and Carmine, my grandchildren, so sweet and full of love: I adore each of you and thank God for sending each of you to our family!

Bobbie Concetta, my adorable, fun-loving niece: I know that Daddy and Harold and Grandma Bacon are watching over you from there as we are watching over you from here. I love you so very much, and I always will.

Gianna, Julia, Nicolas, Shane—all the many children I have been so lucky to have call me Aunt Con: I love you all and wish for God to protect you and make all your dreams come true. I love you all very much.

To my publisher Carrie Kania and to Michael Morrison, thank you always for saying yes. And to my team at HarperCollins: Cal Morgan, Jennifer Civiletto, Hope Innelli, Nicole Reardon, Jennifer Hart, Alberto Rojas, Carolyn Bodkin, Samantha Hagerbaumer, Dori Carlson, Justin Dodd, and Melissa Bobotek, thank you always for your hard work and for introducing my books to the world. I love you all.

Debra Casha, my dear friend: I value our many years of friendship; we go back to childhood together. Both you and Larry will be held in my heart forever. John and I love spending time with you both and look forward to many more years of adventures. I love you both very much.

Richard Arlook: what can I say, from the first time I met you I knew you were a mensch. I will forever be in debt to you for all your help. Thank you from the bottom of my pancreas.

To my many clients who have shared their lives and families and stories with me, I am eternally grateful and will be so forever. Thank you for believing me and caring about me. I will promise to always care about all of you. With my love.

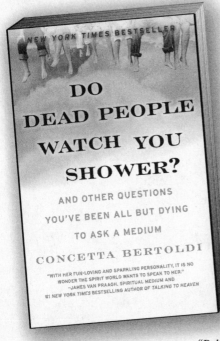